Art with Anything

52 Weeks of Fun with Everyday Stuff

BY MARYANN F. KOHL

DEDICATION

For Hannah and Megan, the "jump-down sisters"!

ACKNOWLEDGMENTS

Fine teachers from around the United States and Canada contributed art ideas and suggestions for everyday materials in *Art with Anything,* inspiring the development of unique activities for children's creative expression. Thank you one and all for your dedication to children's art, your inspiring art ideas, and your generous contribution of time and energy.

Barbara Zaborowski, Phoenix, AZ
Beth Engelhardt, Trotwood, OH
Courtney Price, Lynden, WA
Donna Hooper Moyer, Suwanee, GA
Jane Phelan, Arlington, VA
Karen Heller, Janesville, WI
Katie Dupree, Bel Air, MD
Lisa Skeen, Summerfield NC
Margaret Mahawold, Golden Valley, MN
Melva Herman, La Loche, SK, Canada
Pat Stull, Brandon, FL
Rana Snow, Albany, OR
Sara Kreutz, Holstein, IA
Suzette Milam-Morrow, Cambria, CA
Tracey Neumarke, Chicago, IL
Valerie Kowaluk, Summit, IL
Zannifer Van Antwerp, Henderson, NV

Thank you in particular to three special friends at Gryphon House: Kathy Charner and Kate Kuhn for masterful editing, and Cathy Calliotte for inspired marketing. I treasure your friendships and appreciate your belief in my ability to bring art to children. Working with you is one of the greatest pleasures in my life.

ADDITIONAL BOOKS WRITTEN BY MARYANN F. KOHL AND PUBLISHED BY GRYPHON HOUSE, INC.

First Art
Primary Art
Preschool Art
Preschool Art: Clay and Dough
Preschool Art: Collage
Preschool Art: Craft and Construction
Preschool Art: Drawing
Preschool Art: Painting
Making Make-Believe
MathArts, with Cindy Gainer
Cooking Art, with Jean Potter
Global Art, with Jean Potter

ADDITIONAL BOOKS WRITTEN BY MARYANN F. KOHL, PUBLISHED BY BRIGHT RING PUBLISHING, INC. AND DISTRIBUTED BY GRYPHON HOUSE, INC.

Discovering Great Artists, with Kim Solga
Good Earth Art, with Cindy Gainer
Great American Artists for Kids, with Kim Solga
Mudworks
Mudworks, Bilingual Edition
Science Arts, with Jean Potter
Scribble Art
Storybook Art, with Jean Potter

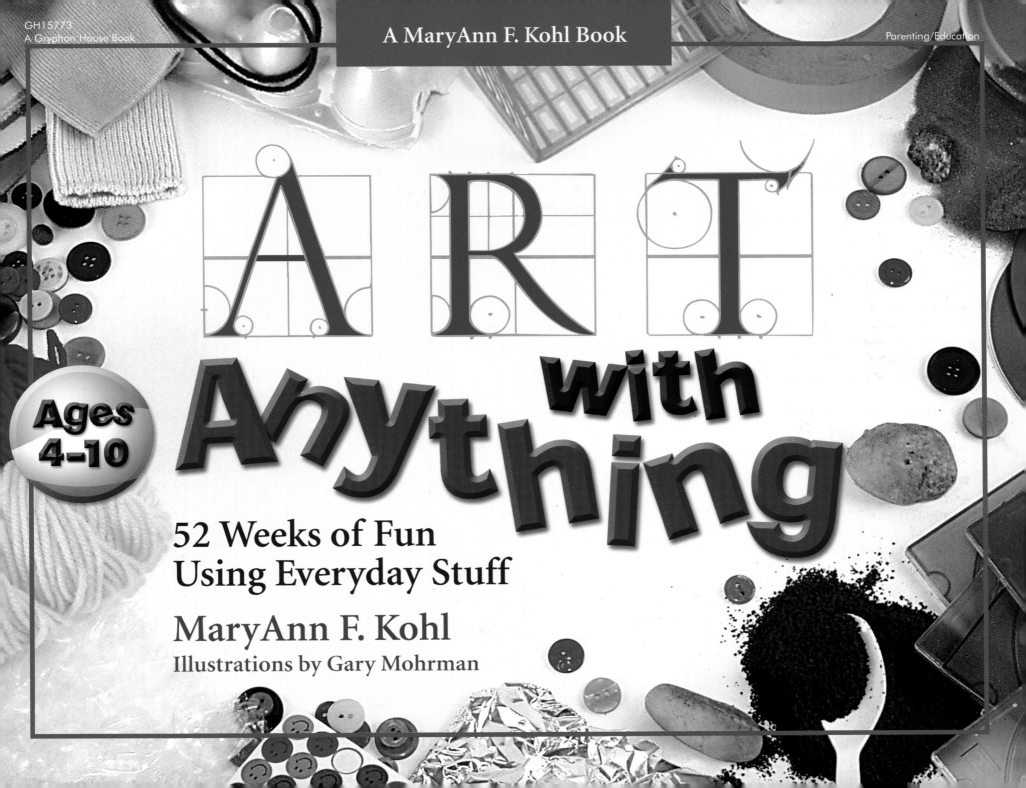

GH15773
A Gryphon House Book

A MaryAnn F. Kohl Book

Parenting/Education

ART with Anything

Ages 4-10

52 Weeks of Fun Using Everyday Stuff

MaryAnn F. Kohl

Illustrations by Gary Mohrman

© 2010 MaryAnn F. Kohl
Printed in China through Asia Pacific Offset, April
2010. This product conforms to CPSIA 2008.

Published by Gryphon House, Inc.
10770 Columbia Pike, Suite 201
Silver Spring, MD 20901 | 301.595.9500
301.595.0051 (fax); 800.638.0928 (toll-free)

Visit us on the web at www.gryphonhouse.com.

LIBRARY OF CONGRESS CATALOGING-IN-PUBLICATION DATA

Kohl, MaryAnn F.
 Art with anything : 52 weeks of fun with everyday
stuff / MaryAnn F. Kohl; illustrations, Gary
Mohrman.
    p. cm.
 ISBN 978-0-87659-085-0
1. Handicraft. 2. Art--Study and teaching
(Preschool) 3. Art--Study and
teaching(Elementary) I. Title.
 TT157.K547 2010
 745.5--dc22
                    2009036427

BULK PURCHASE

Gryphon House books are available for special premiums and sales promotions as well as for fund-raising use. Special editions or book excerpts also can be created to specification. For details, contact the Director of Marketing at Gryphon House.

DISCLAIMER

Gryphon House, Inc. and the author cannot be held responsible for damage, mishap, or injury incurred during the use of or because of activities in this book. Appropriate and reasonable caution and adult supervision of children involved in activities and corresponding to the age and capability of each child involved, is recommended at all times. Do not leave children unattended at any time. Observe safety and caution at all times.

Every effort has been made to locate copyright and permission information.

7/10
BLT

TABLE OF CONTENTS

ABOUT **ART WITH ANYTHING**

The art activities in this book are written for exploration and enjoyment by young artists ages 4–10 at home, at school, in childcare, in after-school programs, or anywhere children have the materials and opportunities to be creative. The 260 art experiences in **Art with Anything** promote the process of art exploration and discovery for each artist regardless of age, experience, or ability. The art activities are written to encourage children to express their creativity, not to reflect a pre-made adult sample or copied mock-up.

To begin, **Art with Anything** is organized alphabetically by everyday materials. Each week focuses on one of 52 common, everyday materials, providing creative art for an entire year, all 52 weeks! For example, the everyday material for Week 1 is Address Labels, Week 2 is Aluminum Foil, and so on until Week 52, which highlights Zip-Close Plastic Bags. Follow the weeks in the order they are listed, or work with any week at any time of the year. It's a good idea to mark off the weeks that you complete so you know which weeks are left to explore.

Each of the 52 weeks is further arranged in a progression of five art activities to fill that week, one activity per day. The art may be explored five days in a row or used to fit your own schedule. The five art activity days are listed as Day 1, Day 2, Day 3, Day 4, and Day 5. Day 1 is the most basic art exploration and a good introduction to the week's material; the other four days build upon the first, culminating with Day 5. Day 4 is always a special "craft day"—a day to make something that is useful, decorative, or just plain cute! Day 5 is the "fanciest" and most challenging art day. Many young artists look forward to Day 5 as the most exciting project of all, the culmination of the five art days of that week.

As you progress through **Art with Anything,** you will notice that there is an element of repetition in the techniques or types of projects explored each week. For example, you will find numerous collage activities, as well as many variations on the technique of creating mobiles. This is a purposeful strategy that builds an artist's skill, understanding, and creativity. Often a collage experience will occur on Day 1, because collage is an excellent way for young artists to become familiar with a new material and learn how to work with that material. The collage activity becomes the springboard for more involved projects in the following days. In the same way, making a mobile takes a relatively stationary or "flat" material and frees it to be viewed from many sides and in new ways. By repeating techniques like collage and mobile construction with different materials, young artists begin to understand the possibilities of art while improving their skill in manipulating materials in artistic ways. Repetition is a powerful tool for developing children's creativity.

All the art activities in **Art with Anything** value and stress the "process of art," and encourage children to think for themselves about how to use materials to make the art their own. Exploration, discovery, and experimentation are key to each child's creative progress. The final result, end product, or finished outcome of the art is not as important as the process of how it came to be, that is, what the child experienced and learned along the way. The visual results of the art will be unique to each child and will delight and inspire both children and adults!

ABOUT THE A–Z MATERIALS

The materials are listed alphabetically from A–Z, and are found in most schools, centers, or homes. Materials range from Address Labels to Zip-Close Bags and everything in between. Each week contains a list of all the materials necessary for each day, and the index at the end of the book also includes all of the materials. Additional supplies and materials for each week's activities are listed with that week so you can prepare ahead of time.

ABOUT SPECIAL ART SUPPLIES

Most of the supplies and materials used in **Art with Anything** are basic; some are more specialized for art. All of the materials allow young artists to use and develop their imaginations.

Some recommended supplies that may require purchase are:

- art tissue (bright tissue paper that "bleeds" color if moistened, available at craft, hobby, and school supply stores)
- child-safe scissors
- cotton swabs (sometimes called Q-tips® or cotton buds)
- craft buttons (available in many sizes in bags at hobby, craft, and school supply stores)
- craft rice (rice dyed multi-colors for art and craft use; not for eating)
- craft roller or brayer (from hobby, craft, or school supply stores)
- craft wire (comes coated in colors or uncoated, available at hobby or craft stores)
- digital camera (for adult use, and for children to use with supervision)
- duct tape (silver is most common; new colors are available)
- electric iron (consider keeping an old one handy for art use; for use by adults only)
- hobby coating (Mod-Podge® is recommended; many others are available)
- liquid starch (found in the laundry aisle in a gallon container)

- liquid watercolor paint (comes in bottles, available at hobby, craft, or school supply stores)
- mat board (scraps often are available free from picture frame shops, or for purchase from hobby or craft stores)
- paper-punch (hand-held hole punch; craft punches also available)
- permanent markers in various sizes and colors (Sharpie® is one brand)
- play clay (colorful soft Plasticine® modeling clay that does not dry out)
- quality crayons (Crayola® is recommended)
- tempera paint (in liquid and powder form, use either or both; sometimes called poster paint)
- water-based markers (many brands—the common markers children use)

ABOUT PREPARATION AND GENERAL CHILD SAFETY

Planning ahead and preparing a work space will help make art experiences a worry-free fun time. Here are some basic suggestions:

- Cover the art table or floor to prevent stains. Consider covering walls and floors if needed. Coverings that work well: inexpensive plastic party tablecloths, old shower curtains, vinyl tablecloths, wide craft paper, or white butcher paper. Newspaper is a reliable old standby.
- Some people use a painters' drop cloth or roll out an old area rug for extra protection. A plastic tarp is another option.

- The artist can wear a smock or apron, an old T-shirt, or a plastic garbage bag with head and arm holes cut to fit. Some artists dress in "art clothes" (clothing used only for art) for special projects.
- Keep a damp sponge on the table near the artist for quick wipes of fingers and hands.
- Require artists to help clean up after each art project.
- Work outdoors if possible when especially messy projects are planned.
- Artists should learn basic safety and clean-up skills such as:
  - Always ask for help if you need it.
  - Clean up spills immediately.
  - Clean your work space, hands, and supplies when you are finished.
  - Wipe hands before touching other people or property.
  - Do not point scissors at anyone; do not walk around with scissors.
  - Place artwork that needs to dry well out of traffic areas.
  - Remember: "Use a little to begin, then add more."
- Artists should help gather supplies, set up, and clean up—all part of the reality of creative art.

Pick an everyday material and have some fun!

Address Labels

Address labels are an inspiration for art any day of the week!

Materials for Day 1 | full sheet of white address labels (used or new) • drawing materials—choose from: crayons, markers, paints and brushes • optional—old magazines or an old poster

Materials for Day 2 | full sheet of white address labels—used or new • drawing materials—choose from: crayons, markers, paints and brushes • background paper—choose from: drawing paper, construction paper or colored paper, sturdy paper or cardboard, poster board

Materials for Day 3 | full sheet of white address labels—used or new • tempera paint or watercolors, brushes, water • optional—crayons or markers

Materials for Day 4 | full sheet of white address labels—used or new • crayons or markers • scissors • background paper—choose from: drawing paper, construction paper or colored paper, sturdy paper or cardboard, poster board • resealable plastic bag or envelope for storing puzzle pieces

Materials for Day 5 | full sheet of white address labels—used or new • drawing materials—choose from: crayons, markers, paints and brushes • background paper—choose from: drawing paper, construction paper or colored paper, sturdy paper or cardboard, poster board

DAY 1

Label Collage

- Color each individual label on a full sheet of white address labels in a different way. Draw designs on some labels, and cover others with single blocks of color.
- To make a simple label collage, peel and stick the labels on a colorful piece of paper in any fashion, overlapping the labels if desired.
- *Picture Cover Art Idea:* Cover a magazine picture or poster, leaving some of the picture exposed between colorful labels and completely covering other parts of the picture.

DAY 2

Painted Label Art

Note: This art idea is for groups or partners.
- Each child paints, colors, or scribbles over an entire sheet of white address labels with one color.
- The artists then share their labels so everyone has different colored labels with which to work.
- The artists use the labels to make colorful collages.
- *Mosaic Idea:* Cut the labels into smaller squares and create a label mosaic on drawing paper.

DAY 3

Woven Look Painting

- Paint a wash of colors on a large sheet of paper. Don't worry about painting a picture—simply paint colors and shapes. Cover the paper completely.
- When dry, peel and stick labels in a planned pattern, with the labels spaced out in lines and rows (or some other pattern).
- The painting may resemble a weaving when viewed from a distance.
- Color or decorate the labels.

DAY 4

Label Puzzle Craft

- Completely cover a sturdy piece of paper or cardboard with peel-and-stick labels.
- Use large labels for beginning artists, and smaller ones for more accomplished artists.
- Draw a picture on the entire sheet of stickers, ignoring lines and sections.
- To make a puzzle, cut the sheet apart between labels.
- Reassemble the puzzle picture.
- When finished, store the puzzle pieces in a resealable plastic bag, envelope, or small box.

DAY 5

Fancy Spaced-Out Labels

- Draw on a full sheet of blank labels using crayons, paints, or markers. Detailed pictures or freeform designs will work equally well.
- Peel off each drawn-on label, and then reassemble the labels in the same order on a piece of poster board. Leave large spaces between the labels as you put them on the poster board. These spaces will create a larger version of the original piece of art, as well as an optical illusion.
- Some artists like to color or decorate between the labels; others prefer to leave the spaces untouched.

Address Labels

13

Aluminum Foil

Aluminum foil is an inspiring art material because of its shine and its ability to form and hold new shapes.

Materials for Day 1 | aluminum foil—clean, recycled pieces or a full roll in a box • colored art tissue paper, colored paper • thinned white glue in a dish, and a brush • shiny collage items, choose from: sequins, buttons, threads, foil papers, and glitter • scissors • optional—construction paper or blank note card • rags or wipes • old washable markers and 3 or more partially full four-ounce bottles of white glue, to make glue paint

Materials for Day 2 | aluminum foil—clean, recycled pieces or a full roll in a box • pad of newspapers • tape • poking tool, like a dull pencil • scissors • colored tissue paper

Materials for Day 3 | Old Marker Glue Paint, prepared on Day 1 • aluminum foil—clean, recycled pieces or a full roll in a box

Materials for Day 4 | aluminum foil—clean, recycled pieces or a full roll in a box • scissors • colored paper, other paper • tape • thick tempera paints, paintbrushes

Materials for Day 5 | paper—choose from: paper plates, white drawing paper, cardboard, poster board, junk mail, colored paper • scissors • thinned white glue and brush • large square of aluminum foil • dull pencil or dull stick • liquid dish detergent and black tempera paint, brush • soft rag or paper towel

DAY 1

Tissue Paper Foil Collage and Glue-Paint Preparation

- Mix white glue and water to make glue that will be easy to apply with a brush (exact proportions are not important). Spread out a piece of foil on your workspace, shiny side up. Tear colored tissue paper into pieces and strips. Brush some glue that has been thinned with water on the foil, place a piece of tissue paper on the foil, and brush the foil and tissue paper with glue again. Repeat the process. Add more tissue paper pieces, creating new colors where the tissue paper pieces overlap.
- Add shiny objects like sequins, buttons, and shiny stickers. Also consider adding bits of foil papers or threads.
- For a finishing touch, sprinkle a little glitter on the wet artwork. Let the artwork dry overnight. When dry, trim edges of foil, possibly with a fancy edge.
- **Preparation for Day 3: Old Marker Glue-Paint:** This is messy work, so have rags or wipes handy. Remove the colorful felt strips from inside the barrels of three or more old washable markers and insert each strip into a partially full or half-full four-ounce bottle of glue. Replace the caps on the glue bottles. Set aside for two days. The color will leach out and stain the glue. On Day 3 of this week, use the colored glue to squeeze a shiny picture on foil.

DAY 2

Shining Light Design

- Place a large sheet of aluminum foil on a thick pad of newspapers. Tape the foil to the newspaper so it doesn't wiggle.
- Using a slightly dull pencil, poke holes into the foil gently and slowly. Cut the holes to any size, or tear them by hand. Any design works.
- Remove the tape from the corners, and then place the foil in a window so the light can shine through the holes.
- To add color, place colorful tissue pieces over the holes and tape each one in place. Then display the foil art in a window with the tissue facing the outdoors. The holes in the foil will shine with color.

Glue-Paint on Foil

- The Old Marker Glue-Paint from Day 1 is now colorful and ready to use.
- Remove the felt strips from the bottles, and replace the caps.
- Squeeze the stained glue from the glue bottle directly onto a square of aluminum foil, making a colorful shiny design.
- Make as many glue designs as you wish. Dry overnight. The glue-paint will become shinier, more colorful, and clearer the longer it dries, so drying for a few extra days is a good idea.

Easy Foil Print

- Cut a piece of foil so it is a little bigger than a sheet of colored paper. Tape the foil to the table.
- Using thick tempera paint, quickly paint a design or picture on the foil. (The paint should be thick so it won't dry too fast.)
- Place a piece of colored paper over the painted foil picture and pat or rub gently to pick up the paint print.
- Remove the paper to lift the print. Set aside to dry.
- **Handprint Foil Idea:** Fingerpaint on the foil or make handprints on the foil (press hand to print on foil, print from foil to paper).

Fancy Foil Relief

- Cut out many shapes from papers of varying thicknesses, such as drawing paper, paper plates, paper from junk mail, or any other paper.
- Glue the shapes on a 20" x 20" piece of cardboard. (If the foil width is less than 20", begin with a smaller square of cardboard for the base.)
- Overlap the paper shapes, layer them, or stack them on the cardboard. Glue everything together.
- Brush white glue thinned with water all over the cardboard and the paper shapes.
- Cover all this with a large square of aluminum foil, shiny side up. Use a piece of foil large enough to wrap an inch or two around all sides of the cardboard. Press the foil down, and the patterns created by the paper shapes will appear.
- Use a dull pencil or other dull stick to indent simple patterns or little shapes on any parts of the foil where there are no paper shapes. Work carefully so the foil does not tear.
- Mix a few drops of liquid dish detergent with black tempera paint to help the paint adhere to the foil. Then brush the black paint all over the foil from edge to edge and let the paint dry.
- With a soft rag or paper towel, lightly rub the surface of the foil to remove black color from the tops of the patterns created by the paper shapes and pencil indents.

Aluminum Foil

Berry Baskets

Plastic berry baskets begin as containers for delicious fresh berries and end as recycled art. Use for prints, baskets, and even a snowflake!

Materials for Day 1 | plastic berry baskets • non-drying playclay or modeling clay (Plasticine®, Plastina®) in many colors • optional—homemade Salt Dough, page 90

Materials for Day 2 | plastic berry baskets • scissors • white glue in a shallow container • glitter, or sand or salt • loop of yarn and paper clip

Materials for Day 3 | tempera paints, paintbrushes • grocery tray for each color of paint • plastic berry baskets • choice of paper • optional—decorating materials: fabric strips, sponge pieces, plastic bag strips • tub with water and liquid soap for bubbles

Materials for Day 4 | ribbon or other weaving material • scissors • plastic berry baskets • glue • optional—strip of cardboard for handle • lace or sewing trim basket filler—choose from: crinkled paper, cotton balls, Easter grass, colorful tissue

Materials for Day 5 | plastic berry baskets • decorating materials—choose from: magazine or comic pictures, gift wrap, art tissue, glitter, hole punches • thinned white glue, brush • optional—art tissue squares, liquid starch

DAY 1

Squash-Clay Basket

- Wash and dry a plastic berry basket. Choose an assortment of colors of playclay, the brightly colored, non-drying Plasticine® variety.
- Make small balls of clay. Gently press a ball of clay from the inside of the basket so it pushes through the holes to the outside. Fill all sides of the basket, including the bottom, with balls of playclay. The clay pieces will eventually press together, filling all the holes and covering all sides of the basket. (The basket can hold dry items like paper clips or other objects when complete.)
- If you don't have playclay, make your own Salt Dough (the recipe is on page 90) or any homemade air-drying dough. Color it with food coloring, tempera paint, or liquid watercolors. After making the dough, repeat the steps above.
- *Snakes and Coils Idea:* Instead of balls of clay, experiment with rolled snakes or coils to press on the basket.

DAY 2

Berry Basket Snowflake

- Ask an adult to cut away the bottom of a plastic berry basket. Make extra snips to create a snowflake shape, or use the square as is. You can cut the sides of the basket to make additional snowflakes.
- Spread all the basket sections on a covered workspace. Brush or dip a basket section with white glue and then dip in glitter. No glitter? Use sand or salt. Let dry until the glue is no longer drippy.
- Carefully turn the section over and repeat the process. Do this for all the snowflake sections.
- When the snowflakes are completely dry on both sides, ask an adult to help attach a loop of yarn or an un-bent paper clip as a hanger. Hang with fishing line, yarn, or thread to create "falling" snowflakes.

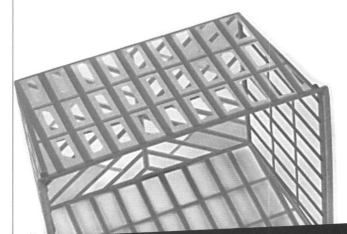

Berry Basket Prints

- Use several colors of paint. Pour each color into a separate plastic grocery tray. Put one berry basket in each color of paint.
- Use the berry baskets to create prints on paper.
- Make single prints or overlap prints.
- *Fun Basket Print Idea:* Poke things like fabric strips, sponges, plastic bag strips, or any other material through the holes in the berry baskets. Dip or drag in paint and make prints.
- *Basket Bubbles Idea:* Fill a plastic tub with water and liquid soap to make a bubble mixture. Dip a plastic berry basket in the bubble mixture, and then wave the basket gently in the air to make tiny bubbles. Mix some paint with the bubble mixture, and the bubbles will make prints when they pop on plain paper. **Note:** Like any paint, bubble paint mix can stain clothes.

Note about berry baskets: If you cannot find berry baskets at your local grocery store or fruit and vegetable stand, there are many websites that sell berry baskets including www.partyfavors4sale.ecrater.com and www.containerandpackaging.com.

Weave a Basket Craft

- Choose a weaving material, like ribbon. Ask an adult to help you cut at least six lengths that are long enough to go all the way around the basket, leaving an additional 2" on each end.
- Begin weaving from a bottom inside corner of the basket, going under and over the mesh spokes. "Under, over" is a common weaving style, but you can use any pattern, including random weaving styles. Try to end inside the basket if possible. With a little glue, press the ribbon down to give it a finished edge.
- Begin weaving another piece of material through the next row of the basket, and continue until you finish weaving material through all the rows. Use all the same material or use different materials for each row.
- If you want a basket with a solid bottom, line the bottom of the basket with a piece of construction paper or cardboard, cut to fit.
- Consider adding a handle of thin cardboard (from a cereal box, magazine cover, or postcard) that an adult can help staple or glue in place. Color the handle with markers or decorate using glue and weaving material. Other handle ideas include ribbon with wire built in, pipe cleaners, and raffia.
- To finish the basket, glue lace or sewing trim around the basket rim. Fill the basket with crinkled paper, cotton, or any lightweight useful item.

Fancy Berry Basket

Choose one of the following techniques to cover a berry basket:

- *Paper Collage Basket Technique:* Cover the work space with newspaper or a plastic tablecloth. Turn a berry basket upside down on a sturdy support, like a block of wood or short jar. Paint the outside of the entire basket with white glue thinned slightly with water. Press strips or squares of comics, gift wrap, or magazine pictures into the glue, covering the basket completely. Also consider covering the interior of the basket. Cover the top edge too! Allow the basket to dry overnight to a hard, shiny result.
- *Art Tissue Basket Technique:* Repeat the preceding technique, but use colorful art tissue squares or strips to decorate the basket. Overlapping the tissue is best so no holes are visible. The basket will have a stained-glass look when dry. Liquid starch can substitute for white glue. **Note:** This basket may not hold small items because the mesh may be open. See suggestions listed at the end of Day 4.

Bubble Wrap

Pop! Pop! and POP! Everyone loves the sound and feel of bubble wrap popping! Pop some, pack with some, and use the rest for bubbly art activities.

Materials for Day 1 | bubble wrap—any sizes of air pockets and bubbles • large paper, like newsprint, butcher paper, or wide craft paper from a roll • tape • peeled crayons

Materials for Day 2 | bubble wrap—any sizes of air pockets and bubbles • fingerpaint • paper for making a print • paper for the background • glue • optional—tape, paints and brushes • painted picture still wet

Materials for Day 3 | bubble wrap—any sizes of air pockets and bubbles • tape or glue colorful scraps of paper or art tissue • white glue thinned with water • collage materials —choose from: paper scraps, art tissue scraps, bits of foil, sequins, feathers, yarn, or other choices

Materials for Day 4 | bubble wrap—any sizes of air pockets and bubbles • rolling pin or paint roller • tape • tempera paint in a large tray or baking pan • scissors • googly craft eyes or buttons

Materials for Day 5 | bubble wrap—any sizes of air pockets and bubbles • scrunched ball of bubble wrap • tray of tempera paint large sheet of paper • optional—crayons, scissors, paper, glue

DAY 1

Bubble-Wrap Surprise Rubbing

Note: An adult needs to prepare this bubble wrap surprise-art activity by taping bubble wrap to a tabletop (bubbles up), completely covering the bubble wrap with newsprint or other large paper, and then taping the paper to the table.

- The surprise: Rub a peeled crayon on its side over the paper. Enjoy the pattern of bubbles on the paper that emerges, and the noise of the bubble wrap popping as you rub crayons more firmly over the paper. Use lots of colors!

DAY 2

Bubble-Wrap Print

- Cover a square of bubble wrap (about 12" x 12") with fingerpaint. Mix several colors at once. (Try mixing and exploring the primary colors: red, blue, and yellow.)
- Place a piece of paper on top of the painted bubble wrap and gently press down. Lift the paper to see the print. Let both the paper and the bubble wrap dry. Glue the dry painted bubble wrap on a larger separate sheet of paper with the bubble–paint side up, and then tape the bubble-wrap print next to the bubble wrap so you can see both pieces together.
- *Bubble Wrap Painted Print Idea:* Use tape to cover a table top with bubble wrap. Paint any color or design on the bubble wrap with tempera paints and paintbrushes. While the paint is still wet, make a print by pressing a piece of paper down on top of the painting and then lifting. The more paint and colors there are on the bubble wrap, the more interesting the prints.
- *Bubble Wrap Smoosh Idea:* Paint a picture with wet, colorful areas. While the paint is still wet and in puddles, place a piece of bubble wrap over the artwork and smoosh it down onto the wet paint. Set the painting aside to dry for an hour. Pull off the bubble wrap to see the patterns left in the dry paint beneath.

Bubble-Wrap Collage

- Use bubble wrap as a unique base for a translucent collage. Pop all the bubbles first (fun!) to make a flat collage, or leave the bubbles puffy. To begin, tape a square of bubble wrap to a flat workspace.
- Tape or glue colorful scraps of paper or art tissue to the bubble wrap. A colorful approach is to use a brush to "paint" art tissue scraps to the bubble wrap with white glue that has been thinned with water. Add more collage items. Be sure everything is secure before moving the bubble-wrap collage and displaying it. Collages can be heavy! Display the bubble-wrap collage in a window to see how the light shines through.

Bubble-Wrap Fish Craft

- Wrap bubble wrap around a rolling pin or a paint roller. Use tape to secure the bubble wrap, bubble-side out.
- Roll the bubble wrap in a tray of tempera paint and then onto paper. When the paint is dry, use this paper to create tropical fish. Cut out colorful paper fish in all shapes and sizes (the bubble dots makes great "scale" marks). Cut out some of the dots to make air bubbles for the fish.
- Make more fish by pressing your hand onto a piece of bubble wrap that has been covered in paint, and then making a handprint, fingers closed together, thumb sticking up on a sheet of paper. Add a wiggly craft eye or button for a fish eye.
- When all the "hand-fish" are dry, cut them out too, and tape them to windows and walls, or hang them on thread wherever a school of fish would be fun to see.

Bubble-Wrap Mural

Note: Ask an adult to help hang a large piece of paper on a wall. (If you prefer, spread the paper on the floor or on a table, then hang it on the wall when dry.)

- Scrunch a ball of bubble wrap into a fist-sized ball bubble-side out, like a softball. Press it into a tray of tempera paint, and then press it onto the paper. Change colors as desired. Use a new bubble-wrap ball for each color, or use one ball of bubble wrap and mix the colors.
- *Scene Mural Idea:* Use this large sheet of bubbly printed paper to create the background of a mural scene. Consider these ideas for the mural backdrop: a forest, an undersea world, the desert, the night sky, an alien planet, or outer space. While the bubble-printed background is drying, color and cut out figures, people, animals, fish, stars, moons, or other elements. Glue them to the mural background to form the complete scene.

Buttons

Save all your buttons, and ask friends to save theirs too. Every single button, no matter what size or color, is an art treasure.

Materials for Day 1 | buttons • liquid watercolors, regular watercolors, tempera or poster paints, markers or crayons • sticks—choose from: tongue depressors, Popsicle sticks, craft sticks • white glue • optional—display choices: vase or jar, string and paper clip, Styrofoam block, colored paper

Materials for Day 2 | buttons with raised patterns or edges • corks • glue gun (adult use only) or white glue, with extra drying time • paper • soft pad of felt over newspaper, or pad of paper towels • inkpad or stamp pad

Materials for Day 3 | buttons • drinking straws • yarn or thread to tie bundle • embroidery floss or yarn • tape • optional—2 chopsticks

Materials for Day 4 | buttons • colored paper scraps • pencil or crayon • scissors • sticks—choose from: tongue depressors, Popsicle sticks, craft sticks, chopsticks, bamboo skewers • white glue • tomato paste can or small jar to serve as a vase

Materials for Day 5 | flat buttons of different sizes • craft wire • scissors (may need adult help) • block of wood or placemat for display

Button Sticks

- Choose one of the following paints to color several sticks: liquid watercolors, regular watercolors, tempera or poster paints, or color the sticks with markers or crayons.
- Look through the assortment of buttons and choose a few favorites. Line them up on a stick. Move them around to get a pleasing design.
- Glue the buttons to the stick.
- *Double Stick Idea:* When the sticks are dry, turn each stick over and glue more buttons on the other side.
- *Four Display Ideas:* Tie one end of a long piece of string to the stick and the other end to a paper clip for a hanging display; place the sticks in a small clear vase or jar; push the sticks into a Styrofoam block so they stand; or glue the sticks to a sheet of colored paper in a design.

Button-Cork Prints

- Select several buttons that have raised patterns. Ask an adult to use a glue gun to glue each button to the end of a cork. The glue will dry strong and hard very quickly. White craft glue will also work, but will need a little extra drying time. (The button diameter should be about the same as the cork.) Make an assortment of button corks.
- To make prints, place a sheet of paper on a soft pad of felt atop several layers of newspaper or a stack of soft paper towels. Press a "button cork" on a stamp pad, and then stamp the inked button on the paper, gently rocking the button back and forth to catch the design on the edges. It is possible to wipe button corks clean, but it is not really necessary; keep stamping and mixing the colors. If a stamp pad is not available, pour some liquid watercolors or food coloring on a pad of paper towels in a tray. Press the stamp onto the pad of paper towels and then on paper.

Button Straws Mobile

- Take three or four drinking straws (or more) and line them up in a bundle. Tightly tie the bundle in the center with yarn or strong thread. The straws will fan out in a sunburst shape.
- Thread embroidery floss or yarn through the holes of several colorful buttons. Tie or tape each button strand to a place on a straw, filling each straw's length with two or three hanging buttons. You may need a dot of glue to hold the yarn in place.
- After attaching hanging buttons to all the straws, tie a long piece of yarn to the center of the straw bundle and hang it in a highly visible spot.
- *Chopstick Mobile Idea:* Tie or tape two chopsticks together at the center, in a cross shape. Thread yarn through the holes of several buttons, and then attach the threads to the chopsticks. Hang to display.

Button Blossoms Craft

- On scraps of colored paper, draw flower-blossom shapes, such as daisies, pansies, mums, or other blossoms.
- Glue a button in the center of each blossom. Let the glue dry a little and then cut out the blossom.
  Note: Cutting well away from the lines looks very artsy; cutting directly on the lines is fine but it is more difficult.
- Find several sticks of different lengths, such as Popsicle sticks, craft sticks, bamboo skewers, chopsticks, or twigs from outdoors. (If you would like, color the sticks with paint or markers before using.) Tape each blossom to a stick (the stem). Make several flowers! Some artists like to tape paper leaves to the sticks as well.
- Choose some favorite flowers and place them in a clean, dry baby-food jar or tomato-paste can. Glue a few buttons to the vase or completely cover this homemade vase with buttons.
  Hint: Garage sales, yard sales, and thrift stores sometimes have bags of buttons for sale.

Button Stacks on Wire

- Sort buttons into different sizes, from large to small, in piles or cups.
- Cut thin coated craft wire into 12" lengths. (You may need adult help.)
- Stack three or more buttons on the table. Begin with a large button on the bottom and add increasingly smaller buttons on the top. The stack may fall over; it's okay, this is only practice.
- To create a button stack on wire, thread wire through the largest button down through one hole and back up through the other hole. The wire ends will stick up from the top of the large button, like two long wire legs. Push the second smaller button onto the two wire legs. Push it down onto the first button, one wire in one hole, the other wire in another hole.
- Add as many buttons as you like to make a stack on the wire legs. Twist the wires together at the top of the stack to finish. Make as many button stacks as you like.
- Arrange the button stacks on a block of wood or place mat to display.
  Caution: Buttons pose a potential choking hazard.

Buttons

Cardboard

Save large boxes, shoeboxes, packing rectangles, or cardboard of all kinds. Cut boxes apart or use whole, depending on the art activity. From painting to sculpture, cardboard is a versatile everyday art material.

Materials for Day 1 | cardboard • instant coffee crystals • water • 3 small cups • 3 paintbrushes

Materials for Day 2 | cardboard • white glue • brush or fingers for spreading glue • magazine or newspaper pages • aluminum foil • chopstick or other stylus tool, like a dull pencil

Materials for Day 3 | cardboard, 2 squares • scissors • glue • tempera paint in a shallow tray • paper • craft roller (brayer), available at craft and hobby stores

Materials for Day 4 | cardboard box • tape • four sheets of paper, or one long roll of paper • crayons or markers, or paints and brushes • scissors

Materials for Day 5 | cardboard • scissors • paint and paintbrush • tape

DAY 1

Coffee Painting on Cardboard

- Use instant coffee on cardboard to make a fragrant, shiny, earth-tone painting! Mix instant coffee crystals with water in three small cups or dishes. Mix the first very, very dark and strong, the second medium (brown), and the third light (light brown or beige).
- Dip a paintbrush into the coffee, and paint directly on a piece of cardboard. Instant coffee dries to a shiny, earthy color.
- *Corrugated Painting Idea:* Tear away the first smooth layer of cardboard and paint on the bumpy corrugation instead.

DAY 2

Cardboard & Foil Drawing

- Spread glue on a piece of cardboard with your fingers or a brush.
- Cover the cardboard with several sheets of magazine or newspaper pages to make it slightly puffy, spreading glue between layers. Spread glue over the last layer.
- Cover this with aluminum foil, wrapping the foil to the back of the cardboard. Tape the foil to the back of the cardboard to ensure it will hold. Turn the cardboard over (foil side up) and lightly pat the foil to help it stick.
- With a chopstick or other stylus tool, gently draw a design in the puffy foil.

Cardboard Prints

- Cut out two squares of cardboard.
- Cut a shape or design from one square and glue it to the other square. Leave as is or complete the design by cutting out additional smaller cardboard scraps and gluing them to the cardboard square. Let the glue dry until good and strong.
- Once the glue is dry, try either of the following ideas:
  - *Press and Print Idea:* Dip the design into paint in a shallow tray, and then press it firmly on paper to make a print.
  - *Brayer Print Idea:* Roll a craft roller (brayer) or small rolling pin in paint in a shallow tray, and then over the cardboard design to produce an even covering. Then press the cardboard on paper to make a print. Some artists like to press and pat a piece of paper directly on the painted cardboard design, peel the paper away, and lift a print.

Story Display Craft

Note: Find a cardboard box. With adult help, tape all the flaps closed. The top and bottom of the box will be not be used in the story. Each of the four sides will be one part of a four-part story (or four drawings or paintings).

- Cover each side with a sheet of paper, or wrap one long piece of paper all the way around the entire box.
- Make up four steps in a simple story. For example: 1. The dog is sleeping; 2. The dog sees a cat; 3. The dog chases the cat; 4. The dog and cat are friends playing together.
- Starting with one side of the box, paint or draw the first part of the story or scene. Turn the box and draw or paint the next part. Do this for all four parts of the story sequence. Include the written story on the drawings, if you like. When complete, walk around the box to view the story from side one to side four.
- *Zigzag Screen Idea:* Cut the box apart to stand in a zigzag accordion fashion like a folding screen to display the four parts of the story. (For stability, cut away the top, but use the bottom flaps to help the box stand). Some artists like to make a story with three parts, and save one side for a decorated title page.

Cardboard Multi-Square Paintings

- Cut cardboard into nine matching squares of any size. (Suggestion: 6" x 6" is a good all-around size.)
- Paint each square a different way. Think about choosing an overall theme for the paintings like: solid colors only, squiggles and lines, geometric shapes, faces, flowers, and so on.
- Once you decide the theme, begin to paint and make each square a different design in the theme. For example, make nine different flower squares, or nine wiggly design squares, nine geometric design squares, or nine cat paintings.
- When the nine squares are dry, join them together by taping them together on their back seams. Taping three across by three down will make one large square of the nine paintings. Also consider taping the nine squares in a long row to make one long line of paintings. How you join the squares together creates the final shape.

Cardboard

Cardboard Tubes

Cardboard tubes from paper towels, gift wrap, and other products are strong enough to support rolled prints, sculptures, and mobiles.

Materials for Day 1 | cardboard scraps • cardboard rolls or tubes—from paper towels, gift wrap • scissors • glue • tempera paints on a pad of wet paper towels • tray or baking sheet

Materials for Day 2 | cardboard rolls or tubes—from paper towels, gift wrap • decorating materials (see Day 2 for ideas) • glue or tape • yarn • mobile materials (see Day 2 for ideas) • optional—paper towels, liquid watercolors or watercolor paints, paintbrush or spoon, yarn

Materials for Day 3 | cardboard rolls or tubes —from paper towels, gift wrap • square of cardboard • glue or tape • colored craft wire

Materials for Day 4 | cardboard rolls or tubes—from paper towels, gift wrap • aluminum foil • white glue and a brush • decorating materials (see Day 4 for ideas)

Materials for Day 5 | cardboard rolls or tubes—from paper towels, gift wrap • green paper • tape, stapler, or glue • display base—choose from: box, basket, bowl, or can • decorating materials (see Day 5 for ideas) • materials for stuffing tubes: shredded paper, crinkled paper, Easter grass, fabric scraps

DAY 1

Tube Roller Print

- Cut triangles, circles, squares, or odd-shaped 1" or smaller pieces from cardboard and glue them to a cardboard tube, covering the tube with the cardboard shapes. (If you have a long cardboard tube, you may want to cut it into shorter lengths.)
- Pour some tempera paint (use one color or many colors) on a pad of wet paper towels in a large tray or baking sheet.
- Roll the tube through the paint, and then roll it on a large sheet of paper to make a rolling print. Colors and designs will mix on the paper as you make multiple passes, rolling over the first design.

DAY 2

Paper Towel Tube Mobile

- Decorate a cardboard roll or paper towel tube in any way: with paint, colored paper, wrapping paper, aluminum foil, stickers, fabric scraps, confetti, feathers, or any other material you choose.
- Tape or tie several pieces of yarn to the tube, spacing them out evenly and letting them hang from the tube. Next, decide what to tie to the end of each yarn strand. Some ideas are: pinecones or nature items, cotton balls or collage items, metal spoons or flatware, beads from baker's clay or Fimo®, small toys or collectibles. Choosing is part of the fun!
- Tie one chosen item to each strand of yarn so it hangs from the tube.
- To finish, an adult can thread a long piece of yarn through the tube to make a hanger, and display it where the strings can swing and move in the air currents.
- *Butterflies Idea:* Drip liquid watercolors or food coloring on five or six paper towel squares spread on newsprint. If the towels are slightly moist, the colors will spread out and blend more. You can also paint on the paper towels with watercolor paints. Let the towels dry. Tie each colorful square around its center with yarn to gather it together in a "butterfly" shape. Hang the butterfly shapes from the tube.

Colored Wire Sculpture

- Glue or tape a cardboard tube to a square of cardboard in a standing position. Be sure it is solid. Allow to dry if glued.
- Wrap colored craft wire around the tube, leaving some ends standing out in creative ways, such as curls, zigzags, spirals, and arches. Wrap the tube with colorful crazy wire until satisfied with the design.

Robot Tube Craft

Note: A paper towel tube can be the beginning form for many creations, including animals, angels, dolls, flowers, candles, and numerous characters. Creating a robot is only one idea!

- To make a shiny robot, begin by cutting a piece of aluminum foil to wrap around a cardboard tube. It should be a little wider than the tube, and long enough to wrap completely around.
- Spread glue on the tube and then wrap the foil around it, folding any extra foil into the openings at either end of the tube.
- To create the robot's features, work with scraps of colored construction paper, stickers, magazine clippings, or other ideas and materials on hand. Think about making buttons, switches, or other high-tech features. Glue or tape the features onto the shiny robot tube. Other fun things to add are googly eyes, buttons, and pipe cleaner antennae.

Wild Freedom Tube Garden

- Cover four or five tubes with green paper, using tape or glue. Stand them up in a box, a flat-bottomed bowl, or a basket. If necessary, use tape or glue to help them stand well.
- For the top of each tube, think of a flower blossom to create using materials such as paper baking cups, colorful art tissue, aluminum foil, cellophane, colored paper scraps, fabric scraps, or plastic bags cut into large, flat pieces. Think of new ways to create blossoms.
- Consider adding collage materials to the tube garden, like confetti or feathers. Push or stick some materials into the open hole at the top of the tube, then fluff them out. Think of other materials to cut or gather into blossom forms and tape or tie them to the tube using yarn.
- When all the tubes have blossoms, the garden is in full bloom to enjoy.

CDs (compact discs)

Save CDs from music, software, or computer backups to use with paint, glue, and other everyday supplies. (CDs with labels will work fine, but shiny CDs without labels are best.)

Materials for Day 1 | shiny CDs, used or outdated • tempera paints and brushes • scratching tool—choose from: ballpoint pen, unfolded paper clip, small sticks • yarn, tape, and paper clip for hanging art

Materials for Day 2 | CDs, used or outdated • permanent markers (for example, Sharpie®) • optional—yarn or twine • child's toy record player, aluminum foil • cutouts of letters

Materials for Day 3 | CDs, used or outdated • optional—tempera paints or acrylic paints, paintbrushes • collage materials—choose from: shredded paper, ribbon, faux fur, fabric pieces, and scraps of all kinds • yarn, pins or hooks • cardboard

Materials for Day 4 | CDs, used or outdated • tempera paints in choice of holiday colors paintbrushes • optional—white glue stained blue with food coloring or paint

Materials for Day 5 | CDs, used or outdated • art of the great masters (from the Internet or from books and postcards) • tempera paints or acrylic paints and brushes, permanent markers

DAY 1

Scratch CD

- Coat the entire surface of a shiny CD with your favorite color of paint, or use more than one color. Wait for it to dry completely, which will not take long.
- Choose a scratching tool like a ballpoint pen with the writing point pulled inside, or an unfolded large paper clip. Scratch designs through the paint down to the shiny CD beneath.
- Hang by the paper clip and a little tape and yarn. Hang several CDs from one long wire, or string all the CDs in a row.

DAY 2

Marks & Color CD

- Draw on a CD with permanent markers. Draw circles, lines, designs, pictures, or other ideas all over the shiny CD.
- *Record Player Coloring Idea:* Place a used CD on a child's old-style record player (Fisher-Price toy record players are great for this) and draw with permanent markers as the CD goes around and around. The best part is when the colors are spinning! (If you must protect the record player from stray pen marks, first cover the record area with aluminum foil or a paper plate taped in place.)
- *CD Banner Idea:* Decorate or paint numerous CDs and string them together with strong twine or heavy yarn. Glue letters to the CDs to spell words or a name, like "Happy Birthday" or "Welcome!" String the banner across a wall, doorway, or from the ceiling.

Silly Animal Face CD

- Think of an animal face to create. Leave the CD shiny and unpainted or painted with a color for the animal. If you paint the CD, let it dry completely.
- Use shredded paper and other collage materials to glue animal facial features like ears, nose, eyes, and whiskers to the CD. Animals with round faces like dogs, cats, lions, and elephants work especially well. You can also create human faces and story characters.
- Use pins or hooks to display the CD faces on a wall, glue them to a large sheet of paper or cardboard, or hang the CDs from loops of yarn.

CD Holiday Craft

- Create holiday CD art! Make a CD bunny, snowman, angel, Santa, leprechaun, or other iconic figure or symbol. Use holiday colors to add impact to the craft, like red for Valentine's Day or green for St. Patrick's Day. For the Fourth of July or other patriotic event, paint with red, white, and blue swirls, or paint stars and stripes in similar colors.
- ***Pumpkin CD Idea:*** For Halloween, paint the CD orange or glue an orange circle over the CD and let it dry. Add eyes, a nose, mouth, and teeth using colored paper and glue. Add a green paper stem.
- ***Snowflake CD Idea:*** Stain white glue with blue food coloring or paint, then decorate a shiny CD with the colored glue, dripping it on in a snowflake pattern.

Great Masters CD

- Check out the styles of great masters like Van Gogh, Matisse, and Monet on the Internet, in a book, or in a museum.
- Choose a favorite artist and paint a CD in colors and designs that reflect the style of that great master. For example, a Van Gogh CD might have a circle of swirling blue sky and yellow stars or bright yellow sunflowers. A Matisse CD might be decorated with bold colorful forms like his famous cutout stars and abstract shapes. A Monet CD might have blurred flowers or lily pads on blue water. To create an O'Keeffe CD, paint large flowers or poppies. To create a Jackson Pollack CD, cover the CD with splatters and drips.

CDs (compact discs)

CD Case

The clear plastic jewel cases that music CDs come in are sturdy enough to protect and display original art, become a book, hold a unique greeting card, or become a wall of original art.

Materials for Day 1 | CD case (jewel case, clear plastic) • original painting or drawing to fit inside the CD case • pencil • scissors • glue or tape

Materials for Day 2 | CD case (jewel case, clear plastic) • heavy cardstock • pencil or pen • scissors • crayons, markers • paint and paintbrush • collage materials (see Day 2 for ideas) • optional—ribbon and glue

Materials for Day 3 | CD case (jewel case, clear plastic) • paper squares to fit inside the CD case • drawing and writing tools—choose from: crayons, markers, colored pencils, and a pencil or pen • strip of paper for spine

Materials for Day 4 | CD case (jewel case, clear plastic) • photographs • construction paper • glue • scissors • optional—decorating materials (see Day 4 for ideas)

Materials for Day 5 | at least 3 CD cases (jewel case, clear plastic) • an original artwork for each case • pencil • scissors • heavy duty duct tape • large paper clips • optional—piece of paper long enough to cover 6 CD cases in row, paints and brushes

DAY 1

CD Art Display

- Flip a CD case open and bend one side of the case slightly backwards, standing it on the table like a desk calendar. One side will be flat on the table, and the other side will angle back at a slant. The slanted area will be used for art display.
- Select an original painting or drawing, or make something just to fit the CD case. To fit well, trace the back of the art with a pencil, using the CD case as a template. Then cut out the art on the lines. (The art may need to be trimmed slightly smaller to fit.)
- Fit the art in place on the slanted plastic square area. Glue or tape in place. The art is now on permanent display!

Note: Some artists like to trace the CD jewel case on drawing paper, create their art within the square, cut it out, and insert it in the case. If your CD case does not flip open, simply attach the art on the front of the CD case. Another idea is to display four artworks, one on each of the four sides of the case.

DAY 2

CD Greeting

- To begin creating a birthday, holiday, get well, or "just because" card, outline the CD jewel case on heavy cardstock and cut out the square. Draw or paint a picture or design that expresses your greeting on the cardstock square. Place the square art inside the jewel case, facing out like the cover of a CD.
- On a second piece of heavy paper, write a greeting like "Happy Birthday" or "I Love You" with markers or letters cut from magazines. Don't forget to sign your name! Slip the greeting inside the case. The card is complete, or you may want to decorate it more.
- Decorate the front of the case with collage materials like ribbon, fun-foam shapes, buttons, puzzle pieces, shells, glitter glue, stick-on jewels and sequins, and so on. Some artists like to glue a ribbon from the opening all the way around the CD case and back to the opening again, and then tie the two loose ends to seal the greeting like a gift.

CD Book

- A CD case has four surfaces: a cover, two inside squares, and the back. Write and illustrate a short book using the two inside pages and back (three pages). The front of the CD is the cover, with the title and the names of the author and illustrator.
- Use crayons, markers, colored pencils, or any pencil or pen. CD cases usually have a spine that you can cover with a narrow strip of paper. Write the title of the book on this strip of paper.
- Make a library full of CD books to share and enjoy.

Standing Photo Frame Craft

- This picture frame made from a clear plastic CD case will stand open on a table or shelf, displaying two photographs on the inside squares.
- To make a frame for the photos, cut two pieces of construction paper into squares that will fit into the CD case. Then cut a square out of the center of each of those squares. The cut-away shape could also be a circle or other shape. It's fun to make wiggly instead of straight edges.
- Glue a photograph on the back of the construction paper frame. Use just a dot of glue on each corner and press the photo to stick.
- Attach the framed photos inside the CD case cover by using dots of glue on the corners of the inside area. To decorate the outside area, use original art cut to fit, colored paper, or any paper or other ideas! In addition, the standing frame edges or surfaces can be decorated with buttons, shells, stick-on craft jewels and sequins, wiggly eyes, stickers, glitter, ribbon, or lace. Stand the frame open to view the two pictures inside. Some artists like to cut words from magazines to add to the photo frame.

CD Art in a Row

- You will need at least three CD cases (many more will also work well). Select an important original artwork for each CD case, or make one especially for this activity.
- Trace the CD case, or trace the shape of the cover art that comes out of the CD case, on the back of the artwork. Cut on the lines and trim slightly. Insert the art in the cover of the CD case. Close the case.
- With heavy-duty duct tape, tape an open paper clip on the back of the case as a hook. Make as many CD covers this way as desired. Display the artworks in their cases in a row on the wall, with the edges touching. Make a long row, or form a square display, depending on how many cases are ready to display.
- *Artwork in Sections Idea:* Arrange six or so CD cases in a group, edge-to-edge. Cut one long piece of paper to fit all six. Paint an original artwork on this paper. Cut the artwork into six equal squares, and place one square in each CD case. Hang the CD cases in order on the wall so the complete painting is once again united (similar to a puzzle)!

CD Case

Coffee Filters

Coffee filters absorb and blend color in unusual ways.

Materials for Day 1 | coffee filters, unused, any size • workspace covered with newsprint • coloring method—choose one or more: cotton swabs and liquid watercolors or food coloring • eyedropper and colored water • spray bottle and colored water • washable markers and water with brush • drying area covered with newsprint

Materials for Day 2 | coffee filters, unused, any size • workspace covered with newsprint or plastic tablecloth • masking or transparent tape • washable markers • paintbrush dipped in water, or spray bottle filled with water • drying area covered with newsprint

Materials for Day 3 | coffee filters, unused, any size • cups filled with liquid watercolor paints • scissors • optional—iron, adult use only • drying area covered with newsprint

Materials for Day 4 | coffee filters, regular size • optional—coffee filters, extra large restaurant size • coloring method (choose from methods and materials on Day 1 or Day 2) • masking tape, colored tape, or yarn • scissors • dolls or stuffed animals

Materials for Day 5 | coffee filters, any size • 3 small cups • liquid watercolors or bright food coloring, and water • white paper—choose from: copier paper, printer paper, blank newsprint • scissors • tape or glue • drying area covered with newsprint

DAY 1

Coffee Filter Exploration

- Place the coffee filter on your workspace (a table covered with several layers of newsprint). Try any or all of the following methods to learn about filters and their colorful possibilities. Move finished wet filters to additional newsprint to dry.
  - *Dot and Dab Idea:* Dip cotton swabs in liquid watercolors or food coloring (mixed with a little water), and dab on a dry coffee filter. Try the same idea, dabbing color on a coffee filter that is damp with water.
  - *Squeeze Drops Idea:* Use an eyedropper to squeeze drops of colored water onto a coffee filter. Try several colors.
  - *Spray Color Idea:* Use hand-held spray bottles to mist coffee filters with water that is mixed with food coloring.
  - *Markers Blend Idea:* Draw with washable markers on coffee filters. Paint clear water on the marker lines with a paintbrush, or use a hand mister, to blur and blend the marker lines.

  Hint: Gigantic coffee filters are available at restaurant supply stores, or look through children's arts and crafts catalogs for "Texas filters."

DAY 2

"Magic Moment" Markers and Filters

- Cover a flat work surface, such as a picnic table, with newspaper or a plastic tablecloth.
- Place white coffee filters all over the table, overlapping their edges a little. Flatten and tape down filters to prevent wiggling or blowing away. Draw with washable or water-based markers directly on the coffee filters.
- For the "magic moment," shake little drops of water from a paintbrush on the marker lines, or for an even more impressive and exciting experience, mist marker lines with a hand-held spray bottle of water. Watch the colors blend and spread like magic over the entire table.

Bright Filter Snowflakes

- To make a brightly colored snowflake, fold a coffee filter, making a point at the center of the circle and folded edges on the sides.
- Partly fill small cups or flat jar lids with liquid watercolor paints. Dip the point and edges of a folded filter into different colors of paint. (For muted colors, mix a little water in each cup of paint.) Place the coffee filter on newsprint to dry briefly.
- Without unfolding the coffee filter, snip large holes from the edges and point, leaving intact spaces between the holes. (Save the colorful scraps.) Unfold to view the brightly colored snowflake.
  Note: To flatten the snowflakes, an adult can iron them on low heat—no steam—between pieces of paper.
- Display snowflakes in windows to show off the colors. Use the scraps for other artworks where colorful paper bits are needed.

Coffee Filter Hat Craft

- Make a hat for a doll or stuffed animal using a regular coffee filter and masking tape. Color the coffee filter in any way with watercolor paints or any other coloring method (see Days 1 and 2). Allow to dry.
- When the filter is dry, place the coffee filter over the toy's head. Hold it in place and wrap a long piece of colored tape, masking tape, or colorful yarn around the coffee filter to make a hatband.
- Make a hat for every toy, and have a hat party! Use extra large filters to make hats for everyone.

Double-Dyed Design

- Fill three small cups each about half-full with liquid watercolor paints or bright food coloring mixed with a little water.
- Cut two squares of white paper, each one a little bit larger than the coffee filter. Place one square of white paper on a work area that is covered with newspaper.
- Fold the coffee filter into any kind of fairly small tight triangle or square. Dip a point or an edge of the coffee filter into some color and quickly out again. You can always add more, but soaking it too much makes the filter hard to handle. Keep dipping the coffee filter in colors until it is well saturated with blended shapes, designs, and color.
- Unfold the filter and place on the square of white paper. With both hands, press another square of white paper over the coffee filter for a few seconds to help the color soak into the white paper, making an imprint. Then peel off.
- Tape or glue the coffee filter to one of the squares, and then tape the other square next to it. There will be two sheets of paper, one with a coffee filter and the other with the imprint of the filter.

Coffee Filters

Coffee Grounds

Save coffee grounds to enjoy for an entire week of fragrant, textured art explorations and creations.

Materials for Day 1 | coffee dough ingredients: used, dry coffee grounds, flour, salt, and cool liquid coffee • bowl, cup, spoon or fork • plastic bag for dough storage

Materials for Day 2 | coffee dough ingredients: used, dry coffee grounds, flour, salt, sand, water • bowl, measuring cups, spoon or fork • cookie sheet, 150°F oven • small treasure • optional—toothpick, yarn or string, hammer or block

Materials for Day 3 | coffee dough (see Day 1) • small toys or objects to make impressions in the dough

Materials for Day 4 | used, dry coffee grounds • white glue thinned with water, brush • collage materials: buttons, ribbons, and other materials • construction paper or newsprint, white paper, waxed paper • optional—coffee grounds mixed into tempera paint, construction paper, newsprint

Materials for Day 5 | fingerpaint ingredients: finely chopped or grated soap chips, cornstarch, water, large saucepan, adult use of stovetop, wooden spoon • small containers for paint • dough-coloring materials (see Day 5 for ideas)

DAY 1

Coffee Playdough

- Mix 1 cup used, dry coffee grounds, 1 cup flour, and ½ cup salt in a bowl. Add about ½ cup cool coffee (add only enough liquid coffee to form a dough that holds together and is not sticky).
- Explore as with any playdough. Coffee dough is a fragrant playdough with an interesting texture and color. Store the leftover dough in a plastic bag.

  Hint: Need more grounds? Ask a restaurant to save some in a container that you provide.

DAY 2

Coffee Dough & Treasure Stones

- Mix 1 cup flour, ½ cup salt, ¼ cup sand, and 1 cup used, dry coffee grounds together in a medium bowl. Slowly add ¾ cup water and knead until the mixture is like bread dough. Make any desired creations.
- To save your creations, ask an adult to bake them in the oven on a cookie sheet at 150°F for 15–20 minutes (longer for larger items).
- *Treasure Stones Idea:* To make a Treasure Stone with a surprise inside, pinch off a ball of dough and roll it into the size of a ping-pong ball, or larger depending on the size of the treasure. In the center of the ball, make a hole big enough to hide a small treasure. Seal with extra dough. Let treasure stones air-dry for 2–3 days or until hard. It is fun to hide the Treasure Stones. When someone finds a Treasure Stone, that person gently cracks it open on newspaper with a hammer or rock to see what is hidden inside. "Treasures" to hide inside a Treasure Stone include a coin, a colorful button, or a small toy.
- *Beads Idea:* Make stone-shaped beads and poke a hole in them with a toothpick. Let the beads dry, and then string them on yarn or thread to make a necklace.

DAY 3

Coffee Impressions & Fossil Slabs

- In a bowl, mix together 1 cup used, dry coffee grounds, 1 cup flour, ½ cup salt, and about ½ cup cool coffee (add just enough liquid coffee to form a pliable dough). Knead the dough and then flatten on waxed paper.
- Use a butter knife to cut slabs of dough large enough to make impressions with objects.
- Press objects firmly into the dough to make impressions. Let the slab dry overnight. When dry, imagine that the slab of dough is rock and the impressions are from fossils.

DAY 4

Fuzzy Bear Coffee Craft

- Use a brush and white glue that has been thinned with water to paint the shape of a bear (or other fuzzy furry creature) on paper.
  Note: You can use a pre-cut pattern of a bear, but your own bear designed entirely by you is more creative, interesting, and valuable.
- Sprinkle coffee grounds on the glue. The bear will be "fuzzy" and brown. Use collage items to add other features, like buttons for eyes and a ribbon to make it look like a stuffed toy bear.
- *Coffee Grounds Paint Idea:* Mix coffee grounds directly into tempera paint, and paint a bear on construction paper or newsprint. Decorate your bear, if desired.

DAY 5

Homemade Fingerpaint with Coffee Grounds

- **Reminder:** Today is the day to crack open the Treasure Stones from Day 2.
- **Adult Step:** Combine ½ cup finely chopped or grated soap chips, 1 cup cornstarch, and 6 cups water in a saucepan. Bring to a boil over medium heat, stirring constantly. Remove when thickened. Pour into individual containers.
- Place one color of crushed chalk, powdered tempera paint, or liquid watercolor paint in each container and mix while still warm. Let cool. Add texture with coffee grounds. Add fragrance, choosing from vanilla, cinnamon, perfume, or liquid hand soap. Store in covered containers.
- Use the liquid as you would any fingerpaint: Place a dollop on paper and smear it with your hands and fingers.

BONUS IDEA:

Coffee Paper

Materials
used coffee grounds
pan of water
paper
newspaper or old towel

Place used coffee grounds in a pan of water and let them soak until the water turns a rich brown. Slip a sheet of plain paper into the tray until it becomes stained brown. Gently remove the paper from the tray and allow it to dry on newspaper or an old towel. The effect of using coffee grounds creates paper that looks like parchment or antique document paper. Use coffee paper for any of this week's art activities, or use for thank-you notes, antique maps, or other paper uses.

Coffee Grounds

Contact Paper

Contact paper is also called self–adhesive vinyl. It comes clear or patterned, with peel-off backing. Some large pieces are necessary for a few of this week's projects, but small pieces are valuable treasures to save for sticky-based art explorations.

Materials for Day 1 | contact paper (self-adhesive vinyl, clear or patterned) • collage materials—choose from: confetti, glitter, sand, salt, craft rice, strands of yarn, hole-punch dots, and other materials

Materials for Day 2 | contact paper (self-adhesive vinyl, clear or patterned) • natural materials—choose from: leaves, grasses, weeds, twigs, blossoms • optional—non-natural materials, like yarn or confetti

Materials for Day 3 | contact paper (self-adhesive vinyl, clear or patterned) • construction paper scraps • optional—scraps of left-over colored coffee filters

Materials for Day 4 | contact paper (self-adhesive vinyl, clear or patterned) • tape • plastic spoon • glitter or confetti, hole-punch dots, and small torn pieces of paper

Materials for Day 5 | contact paper (self-adhesive vinyl, clear or patterned) • tape • newspaper or large sheet of paper • tempera paints • optional—small bits of paper, glitter

DAY 1

Sticky Explore Collage

- Spread a large square of contact paper, sticky side up, on your workspace. Feel and explore the stickiness.
- Completely cover the contact paper with paper scraps and collage materials until the sticky area is filled. Some artists like to cover the areas between paper shapes with colored craft rice, glitter, salt, or sand.

DAY 2

Nature Contact Mural

- Go on a nature walk and collect all kinds of natural materials, like grasses, twigs, blossoms, and weeds.
- Press and stick the natural discoveries on a large sheet of contact paper (mounted on the wall, sticky side out). Add other materials for color and design, like yarn strands or confetti, if you like.

Sticky Drop Collage

- Spread contact paper on the floor, sticky side up. Stand on a low stool, sturdy kitchen ladder, steps, or even an outdoor climber (ask an adult to help you do this).
- Tear strips and scraps of construction paper (see leftover paper, Day 3 of Coffee Filters on page 31) and let the pieces fall and stick to the contact paper.
- Repeat the process, until you are satisfied with the finished design. After the pieces land on the contact paper, you may want to press the pieces down more securely by hand.

Glitter Pix

- Place contact paper on a table, sticky side up. Secure the corners to the table with tape.
- Use a plastic spoon to sprinkle glitter on the contact paper in a design or picture. Putting glitter in small shakers will also work. Instead of glitter, use confetti, hole-punch dots, or small torn pieces of paper if you prefer. Use one material alone, or combine with others for more variety.

Clean Fingerpaint Smoosh

- Cover a table with a large piece of paper (newspaper works fine).
- Drizzle paint (two or three colors) on the paper.
- Cover the paper and paint with contact paper, sticky side up. Seal all the edges with long pieces of tape.
- For the big fun, create "clean" fingerpainting on the top of the contact paper, pushing the paint about and watching the colors mix. The tactile stickiness combined with the way the paint spreads out is inspiring!
- *Sprinkles Idea:* Sprinkle bits of paper and glitter in the paint and on the paper before covering with contact paper.

Contact Paper

Cotton Balls

The most impressive appeal of cotton balls is their puffy softness. They also absorb color surprisingly well, and—believe it or not—can be made into batter or dough—a very unusual creative art experience.

Materials for Day 1 | cotton balls (bag of the inexpensive cosmetic variety) • white glue in a shallow container • construction paper, paper plate or other background paper

Materials for Day 2 | cotton balls (bag of the inexpensive cosmetic variety) • scissors • cotton ball clay ingredients and materials: flour, water, cotton balls, bowls, saucepan, spatula, measuring cups, stove (adult use only) • optional—newspaper balls or other base

Materials for Day 3 | cotton balls (bag of the inexpensive cosmetic variety) • glue • original crayon drawing

Materials for Day 4 | cotton balls (bag of the inexpensive cosmetic variety) • scissors • twig or small branch • construction paper • white glue • optional—vase or can

Materials for Day 5 | cotton puff batter ingredients and materials: cotton balls, flour, water, mixing bowl and spoon, food coloring, oven (for adult use only), cookie sheet, cooking spray, spatula • optional—marker

DAY 1

Basic Cotton Ball Exploration

- Explore creating a basic collage by dipping cotton balls in a jar lid of white glue, and then pressing the cotton balls onto a paper plate or other background material. Add other on-hand materials to the collage.
- For an additional fun color experience, first dip cotton balls in a small amount of powdered tempera paint, then in glue, and then stick the cotton balls to the chosen background or paper plate.

DAY 2

Cotton Ball Clay

- Tear or snip 3 cups cotton balls into small pieces.
- **Adult Step:** Mix 2 cups water and the cotton ball pieces together in a medium saucepan, and then slowly stir in ⅔ cup flour so the mixture does not get lumpy. Continue stirring over low heat for about five minutes until the mixture begins to stiffen. Remove from the heat and place the cotton clay on several layers of paper towels to cool.
- When cool, mold this clay into shapes and small sculptures. Dry for 24 hours or until rock hard.
- *Cotton Mâché Idea:* Cotton Ball Clay can be used like papier-mâché to mold around balls of newspaper, a frame, or other base.

Pulled Cotton Fill Drawing

- Cotton wisps are excellent for filling in shapes in an artwork. The cotton might be used as clouds, hair, fur, snow, or simply an abstract texture in any drawing.
- Pull cotton balls apart into thin wispy pieces.
- Using just a tiny bit of glue, cover parts of a crayon drawing with the cotton pieces.

Cotton Ball Blossom Craft

- Cut cotton balls in half or quarters.
- Glue a large twig flat on a sheet of construction paper.
- Glue pieces of cotton balls to the branch to make blossoms or pussy willows.
- *Branch Drawing Idea:* Draw a branch on paper instead of starting with a twig. Glue the blossoms to the drawing.
- *Blossom Branch Idea:* Glue cotton blossoms to a larger branch and display it in a vase or can.

Cotton "Odd-Ball" Puff Batter

- **Adult Step:** Pre-heat an oven to 300°F, spray a cookie sheet with cooking spray to prevent sticking, and then set it aside.
- **Make the Cotton "Odd–Ball" Puff Batter:** Pour 1 cup warm water into a large mixing bowl and add 1 cup flour, mixing slowly until all of the flour is mixed in. Divide the mixture into two or more small bowls; add food coloring to each bowl to color the batter. For more color, make more batches of the mixture and divide and color as desired.
- Dip a cotton ball into colored batter. Push it down under the batter and roll it around until well-covered. Pull it out and place it on the cookie sheet. Keep dipping cotton balls in the various colored mixtures. Place them on a cookie sheet in any design with the battered balls touching.
- Ask an adult to bake the puff designs for one hour; cool slightly and then remove with a spatula.
- **Optional:** Decorate the baked cotton art with markers.

Cotton Balls

Cotton Swabs

Cotton swabs have many names, like cotton buds or Q-Tips®, and are fun to use for art activities. Discount stores often carry pastel-colored swabs.

Materials for Day 1 | cottons swabs (Q-tips®, cotton buds) • markers, water-based • white paper • water in cup

Materials for Day 2 | cottons swabs (Q-tips®, cotton buds) • tempera paints in several colors • grocery tray or paper plate • white paper, several sheets per person • pencil

Materials for Day 3 | cottons swabs (Q-tips®, cotton buds) • liquid watercolors, food coloring mixed with water, or tempera paints • newspaper for drying • yarn • scissors

Materials for Day 4 | cottons swabs (Q-tips®, cotton buds), a handful per snowflake • waxed paper • white glue in squeeze bottle • optional—glitter • thread, embroidery floss, or fishing line for hanging from paper clip

Materials for Day 5 | cottons swabs (Q-tips®, cotton buds) • liquid watercolors or tempera paints • cups, jar lids, or muffin tins for paints • newspaper or aluminum foil for drying area • Styrofoam packing block • paintbrush • optional—embroidery floss

DAY 1

Swabbed Color Lines

- Draw on white paper with water-based markers.
- Before the marks dry, dip a cotton swab in water and trace over the marks. The marks will "bleed" and blur.
- Draw more lines, and repeat the water-and-swab technique. Go back over any dry lines, adding more water.

DAY 2

Dot Painting

- Pour small puddles of several tempera paint colors on a plastic tray from the grocery store or a paper plate.
- Dip a cotton swab in paint, and then make dots on a sheet of drawing paper. Experiment with dots touching or mixing. Then set the experiment aside.
- Use a pencil to draw a simple picture lightly on a piece of paper. Think about how to fill in the drawing with dots of color using cotton swabs and tempera. It may take a while to "color in" the drawing with dots of paint. If the painting dries out, you can add more dots later.

Festive Swab Garland

- First dip cotton swab buds into paint or food coloring to color the white tips. Be prepared to use a lot of cotton swabs, so color quite a few! You can also stain the sticks with color. Consider leaving some swabs white for contrast. Dry the cotton swabs on newspaper.
- Meanwhile, cut yarn into 6"–12" lengths. Use one color or a combination of colors.
- Cross two colored swabs. Tie the center where they cross with a strand of yarn. There should be plenty of extra yarn hanging from each cross. Repeat this process, making many swab-crosses.
- To make a garland of swab-crosses: Tie one to another until you have a continuous garland of colorful swabs.

Cotton Swab Snowflake Craft

- Spread a sheet of waxed paper on a flat workspace. With a handful of cotton swabs (10–20 and probably many more), create a snowflake design on the waxed paper. Swabs can be used whole, bent or broken, but should always connect and touch. Real snowflakes are six-sided, but feel free to be creative with these snowflakes.
- When the design is ready, squeeze plenty of glue over each joint. Don't worry if the glue blobs out and looks messy, because it will harden clear and look more crystallized this way.
- **Optional:** Sprinkle glitter on the glue before it dries. Allow the snowflake to dry on the waxed paper overnight or for at least four hours. Make one snowflake or many snowflakes.
- When the glue has dried completely, very slowly and carefully peel the snowflake from the waxed paper. If the snowflake breaks, put it on the waxed paper again and add more glue. Dry again and peel when dry.
- Hang snowflakes with thread, embroidery floss, or fishing line. An unbent paper clip makes a simple hook for hanging.

Swab the Deck

- Fill shallow cups, muffin tins, or jar lids with a choice of paint in various colors. Liquid watercolors are perfect for this project; tempera paint will work fine, although it takes a little longer to dry.
- Dip cotton swabs in various colors and spread them all on newspaper or aluminum foil to dry a little. Some artists like to make each end a different color, others like the one-color approach. The stick part of the cotton swab may also be colored, but plastic ones won't hold the color as well as the paper variety. As the swabs dry, prepare the "deck."
- Place a Styrofoam packing block, the kind that is dense and smooth, on a table. Ask an adult to cut the block into a smaller size, or use as is. Push a cotton swab into the Styrofoam about ½" or so until it stands firmly on its own. Some of the paint will rub off around the hole. Push more swabs into the block, filling it with color and creating a spiky design.
- When satisfied, take a wet paintbrush around the hole of each swab and spread the paint out a little. Let the design dry.
- *Looped Thread Idea:* When dry, gently loop embroidery floss from one swab to another, looping and tying the threads to the swabs. Adult help may be needed.

Cups

Cups can be an inspiration for creative art techniques like painting, printing, or sculpture. Use cups made from paper, plastic, and Styrofoam, or recycled from containers for yogurt, margarine, and cottage cheese.

Materials for Day 1 | yogurt cup • tempera paint • heavy paper plate or a clean grocery tray for paint • construction paper • materials for experimenting (see Day 1 for ideas)

Materials for Day 2 | paper cups • scissors • colored paper or poster board • white glue • pencil for curling • markers

Materials for Day 3 | yogurt cups, or other cups (clear plastic, margarine, cottage cheese) • acrylic paint and sponge or brush • plastic shopping bag or sandwich bag (or surveyors' plastic tape) • scissors • stapler • hole punch • yarn or twine • optional indoor decorations —paper streamers, ribbon, fabric strips

Materials for Day 4 | margarine container with snap-on lid • yarn rolled in ball • scissors • decorating materials (see Day 4 for ideas)

Materials for Day 5 | clear plastic cups • permanent markers • optional—art tissue, or pieces of magazine and catalog pages; thinned white glue or liquid starch and brush • stapler • yarn

DAY 1

Yogurt Cup Circle Print Exploration

- Pour a small amount of tempera paint onto a heavy paper plate or plastic grocery tray.
- Dip the rim of a clean yogurt cup into paint and then press it on a sheet of construction paper to make a circle print. For multiple colors, fill several trays and use a different yogurt cup for each color.
- Experiment with both the top and the bottom of the cup. For more experimentation in printing, try any or all of the following: Roll the cup through paint and then on paper; mix tempera paint with liquid starch or white glue; sprinkle prints with glitter, salt, or sand; use other kinds of cups; print on textured or glossy paper; tape paper to a wall or easel instead of on a flat table.

DAY 2

Paper Cup Collage

- Starting at the top rim of a paper cup, cut down toward the bottom rim. Stop cutting about ½" above the bottom rim; repeat, spacing the cuts at least 1" apart. (The cup will look a little like a daisy with petals when you finish making all the cuts.)
- Glue the cup to a sheet of colored paper or poster board. Cut and glue as many cups as desired.
- Flatten the "petals" of the paper cups, curl them with a pencil, or snip them with scissors in any way.
- Color the cut strips or insides of the paper cups with markers to add design and color.

Windy Cups

- A yogurt cup, or any cup, can become art that blows in the wind outdoors or near an open window indoors. If you plan to use the Windy Cup outdoors, cut out the bottom so water does not collect in the cup.
- To decorate the cup, dab acrylic paint over the cup with a sponge or brush to cover the product pictures and print. Let dry briefly until the cup can be handled.
- Cut strips from a plastic shopping bag or sandwich bag, or cut several lengths of colorful plastic wicky tape (the kind that surveyors use to mark property). Staple the strips to the bottom ring of the cup.
- To make a hanger, punch three or four holes spaced evenly around the top edge of the cup. Thread yarn or twine through each hole. Then bring all the strands together and tie in a knot. Suspend the cup in a windy spot and see the tapes blow.

  Note: You can create an indoor Windy Cup with a paper cup as the base, since it will not be subjected to the elements. For indoor use, you can use paper streamers, ribbon, or fabric strips instead of plastic.

Yarn Dispenser Craft

- Make a useful yarn dispenser. Roll yarn into a ball until it is about 2 ½" in diameter, or just large enough to fit in a margarine container with the lid snapped on.
- Ask an adult to help you poke a hole in the lid of the margarine container with the point of scissors. Thread the loose end of the yarn through the lid from the inside out, with the yarn resting inside the container, and snap the lid on the cup. The yarn will easily pull from the cup when needed, and can be snipped off after each use. Yarn rarely falls back in to the cup. This makes yarn use more independent.
- Make a yarn dispenser for each color of yarn. Decorate the margarine container with acrylic paints or cover it with a collage of gift wrap brushed on with white glue mixed with water. The most fun of this activity is rolling the balls of yarn!

Sensational Plastic Cup Hanging Sculpture

Note: This activity can be done by one artist, or by a group of artists. Each artist can contribute his or her cup to the display.

- Draw and color on the outside of a clear plastic cup with permanent markers (this creates a see-through colorful stained glass look). Brush pieces of art tissue onto the cup, using liquid starch or white glue thinned with water to make the art tissue adhere. Another alternative is to cover the cup with a collage of pictures from magazines or catalogs, brushing the cup with white glue thinned with water and then brushing again over the pictures. Let the cups dry so they are easy to handle.
- Stand one cup beside another cup. Staple the top rim of one cup to the second cup side by side. Staple the second cup to a third cup side by side. Continue in this fashion, stapling cups together until you have a large grouping of cups joined together at the top. The design can go in many directions, from a flat grouping to a blossom look to a chandelier style.
- To display the cup sculpture, thread yarn between several cups and tie above the sculpture to form a hanger. Suspend the sculpture from above with the yarn.

Digital Cameras

Digital cameras offer the speed of viewing photographs almost instantly, as well as the ease of printing them out for multiple uses, including creative art activities.

Materials for Day 1 | digital camera and a computer to view the pictures • make-up or face-paint • optional—hair props: wig, scarf, bandana; printer, to print the pictures from the computer, and printer paper; scissors and glue; crayons or markers

Materials for Day 2 | digital camera and a computer to view the pictures • props to make scenes (toys, dolls, action figures, paper backdrop, and other ideas)

Materials for Day 3 | digital camera and a computer to view the pictures • printer, to print the pictures, and plain paper • scissors • glue or tape • colored paper, cardboard, or scrap of wood • white glue thinned with water, and brush

Materials for Day 4 | digital camera and a computer to view the pictures • blank wall • friends as models • printer and paper • scissors • glue • large sheet of paper

Materials for Day 5 | digital camera and a computer to view the pictures • picture walk outdoors • printer, to print the pictures from the computer • printer paper • optional—scissors, glue or glue stick, paper, notebook, or scrapbook

DAY 1

Upside-Down Funny Face

- Think up a funny "upside down" pose. For instance, hang backwards from a bed, a bench, or an outdoor climber. Pose so your face is upside down with your hair flying out. Another easy pose is to lie on the floor on a plain carpet or sheet with your hair standing out. Fluff out your hair or brush your hair away from your head to look wild and silly. Short hair? No problem! Wear a wig, wrap your head in a scarf, or skip the hair issue entirely. Be sure to make a funny face! Make-up or face painting adds creativity, expressive features, and drama to the face.
- Ask a friend or an adult to take a picture of the pose, zooming in on your face. Then, as soon as possible, look at the pictures on a computer. Upside down faces are really funny!
- *Funny Face Art Idea:* Print out the pictures, and then cut and paste them to a plain piece of paper. Add more design features with crayon or markers.
  Hint: Kids are always interested in anything they can do themselves. With a little patience and encouragement from you, they will feel confident in taking their own digital pictures.

DAY 2

Photo Scene Art

- Choose a few toys to arrange in a single scene that tells a simple story or communicates a message. Design a paper backdrop for the scene too. Choose some other props to add. The scene can come from a story that everyone knows, a new story, or tell a message about something you want to communicate. For example, arrange a toy dog and toy cat in front of empty food bowls to communicate that animals need proper care and feeding to be happy and healthy. Or arrange a blonde doll in a little bed to tell part of the story of "Goldilocks and the Three Bears."
- Take a picture of the scene and then look at it on the computer. Crop the photo as needed.
- Consider adding text to the photo scene to share the story or message.

Photo Name Speller

- Walk around inside or outdoors looking for the letters of your name. Take a picture of each separate letter that you find in signs or on products. For example, Mary might see the letter M on the McDonald's restaurant sign, an A on the front of a magazine like Art for Kids, an R on a cereal box of Rice Krispies®, and the letter Y on the license plate of a car. Mary, with adult help, snaps a picture of each of her letters by zooming in on the letter in each photo.
- Use a computer and printer to print each letter photo (in color or black and white) on plain copier paper.
- Cut out each letter, joining them together to spell "MARY."
- Glue the letters in order on a bright colored-paper background, on cardboard, or on a scrap of wood.
- Paint over all the letters with white glue thinned with water to give the letters a little shine.

Friends & Faces Mix-Up

- Set up a place to take pictures of your friends where each one can stand in front of a blank wall. This way, all the pictures will have the same background and the people will be about the same size in the photo.
- Use the close-up feature of a camera to take a picture of each friend from head to toe so your friend fills the photo. Print out all the photos of your friends.
- Cut the friend photos in half through the middle, or however you choose, but two pieces is usually a good start. Then glue the friends back together on a large sheet of paper, mixing them with other friends. For example, glue a boy's head on a girl's body and boy's legs and feet on a girl's head and shoulders. Or glue the right half of one girl with the left half of another. Glue all the friends mixed and matched until you create new and (often quite silly) mixed-up people.

Picture Walk

- Go on a picture walk, inside or outside. Focus on a single subject or theme. Take pictures of any of the following ideas (or any other idea of your own):
  - *Shapes:* All the triangles or circles that you see.
  - *Special friends or people:* Daddy, best friend, pets, teacher.
  - *ABCs:* Objects from A to Z, from apple to zipper. Or, choose one letter and find many things that begin with that one letter, like B (ball, boy, bark, bathtub, baby, and so on).
  - *Colors or patterns:* A favorite color, only bright red, all kinds of blue, or many kinds of stripes! Choose a color or a pattern of colors to focus on.
  - *Textures:* Things that are "soft" (cotton balls, clouds, Grandma) or "bumpy" things (sidewalk, rocks, placemat).
- Print the pictures on plain copier paper and enjoy them as they are; or, you can cut and paste them into collages, make them into posters, or place them in a notebook or scrapbook. What else might be fun to try?

Duct Tape

Duct tape is intrinsically beautiful on or off of the roll. It is strong and versatile for art activities, from a simple collage to large, permanent sculptures. Silver duct tape is most common, but duct tape also comes in a rainbow of colors.

Materials for Day 1 | duct tape • scissors • background material, choose from: heavy paper plate, square of cardboard, other board • optional materials for coloring (see Day 1 for ideas) • optional—soft cloth

Materials for Day 2 | duct tape • large sheet of newsprint or other plain paper • scissors • coloring method (see Day 2 for ideas) • optional—paper towels

Materials for Day 3 | duct tape • balls of newspaper • tape • collage materials—choose from: yarn, faux fur, feathers, fabric scraps, paper scraps • permanent colored markers

Materials for Day 4 | duct tape • object to cover with duct tape: lunch bag, can, jar, or book • scissors • optional—painters' blue masking tape

Materials for Day 5 | duct tape • object to cover with duct tape: stuffed toy, tea pot, cardboard box, or wood scrap • collage materials—choose from: yarn, faux fur, feathers, fabric scraps, paper scraps

DAY 1

Duct Tape Collage Exploration

- Select a background board like a heavy paper plate, a square of cardboard, or other strong backing. Pull and cut pieces of duct tape from a roll.
- Press and overlap duct tape pieces until you cover the board completely.
- *Crayon Rubbing Idea:* Place a sheet of paper over the duct tape collage. Then rub the paper with the side of a peeled crayon. The bumpy design of the collage will appear on the paper.
- *Shoe Polish Color Idea:* Rub the tape with shoe polish. Then rub the design with a soft cloth to remove some of the color. The polish will adhere to the edges of the tape, giving the design more definition. Or, paint over the duct tape with thin tempera paint. When the paint is almost dry, rub away some of the color.

DAY 2

Duct Tape Spaces

- Place a long piece of duct tape (whatever is manageable, up to about 3'), on a large sheet of newsprint or other plain paper. Add additional pieces of tape. The pieces of tape can overlap, but be sure there are spaces here and there between the tape pieces.
- With markers, crayons, pencils, paint, or liquid watercolors, fill in and color the spaces in between the pieces of tape. Some artists like to draw designs in the spaces, while others like to fill in the spaces with solid color. If using paint, use paper towels to wipe the excess paint from the duct tape when you finish.

Duct Tape Sculpture

- Form balls of newspaper. Tape them together with regular tape, building a shape for a sculpture. The sculpture may be abstract, or it may take on an actual shape, like an animal or a person.
- Cover the entire newspaper form with lengths of duct tape. Cover until the sculpture is strong and completely covered. The sculpture may be decorated with yarn, faux fur, feathers, or fabrics, or add additional features with permanent markers.

Duct Tape Décor Craft

- Cover a book or a lunch bag, a can or a jar, or anything that needs a sturdy cover. Overlap small pieces of duct tape, or use longer pieces to cover large areas more quickly. It is interesting to use two or more colors of duct tape if available. Combining duct tape with masking tape or painters' tape for color is a creative alternative.

Duct Tape Surreal Sculpture

- Find an object that is broken or something that is no longer needed—anything from a stuffed toy to a teapot. Even a small cardboard box or a wood scrap will work. Cover the object with duct tape pieces and strips. Cover the object entirely, or leave some interesting parts uncovered. Add other materials, if desired, like feathers or scraps of colored paper.
- The finished work will reflect the amusing, confusing style of the great Surreal artists who called themselves Dadaists. A good example of this kind of work is Meret Oppenheim's piece, "Object," a fur-lined teacup on display at the Museum of Modern Art in New York City.

Duct Tape

Egg Cartons

Egg cartons come in colorful Styrofoam or pressed paper in blues and grays; both are equally useful for many creative art experiences.

Materials for Day 1 | egg cartons, either Styrofoam or paperboard • collage materials (see Day 1 for ideas) • scissors • darning needle to poke a hole (adult step) • yarn • button • plastic coat hanger • optional—jingle bells • carton pulp preparation: paper egg cartons torn into 1" or smaller squares, large bowl, warm water

Materials for Day 2 | egg cartons, either Styrofoam or paperboard • scissors • lei flower decorations (see Day 2 for ideas) • drinking straw segments • large plastic darning needle and yarn

Materials for Day 3 | pulp prepared on Day 1 (4 cups or more of torn paper egg cartons soaked in water overnight) • adhesive choice: white glue or wallpaper paste • plastic bowl • acrylic paints and brushes, or markers • waxed paper for drying sculptures

Materials for Day 4 | egg carton, either Styrofoam or paperboard • drawing paper, markers or crayons • scissors • glue • Easter grass • cotton balls • scraps of construction paper

Materials for Day 5 | large paperboard egg flat, or 4–6 egg cartons • optional—glue or stapler • variety of tempera paint colors in cups • paintbrushes • optional—duct tape

DAY 1

Egg Carton Mobile

- Cut any kind of egg carton apart, saving all the cups for the mobile, but setting aside other parts to use at another time.
- Decorate the inside and outside of each cup as desired with a combination of paper scraps, glue, glitter, sequins, markers, stickers, yarn, or other collage materials. Dry on newspaper.
- Ask an adult to help you poke a small hole in the center of each cup. Push a strand of yarn through the hole to the inside of the cup and tie a button or scrap of paper to the yarn so that it will hold inside the cup. Next, tie the other end of the yarn to a plastic coat hanger. Do this with all the cups, hanging them from the plastic hanger one by one. Make the yarn different lengths so the cups all hang at different levels, or hang the cups using identical lengths of yarn.
- Fill the hanger with all 12 decorated cups (or any number of cups). Suspend the plastic hanger where air currents will move the hanging cups.
- *Noisy Mobile Idea:* Tie a jingle bell inside each cup on the yarn so the mobile will make a little sound when it moves.
- **Prepare for Day 3:** Take a little time today to tear paper egg cartons into small pieces for Day 3's activity. Tear paperboard egg cartons (or large paperboard egg-carton flats) into small pieces 1" square or smaller. Tear and tear until there is a good bowlful, about 4 cups or more. Pour some warm water over the torn pieces, and let the bowl stand until you need it.

DAY 2

Egg Carton Lei

- Cut any kind of egg carton cups into separate sections (Styrofoam cartons come in pretty colors). 12 egg carton cups will lightly fill one necklace or lei; more than 12 will make a thicker, more colorful result.
- Materials that will work well for imaginary flowers include circles of colored paper, tissue circles or squares, silk flower blossoms, fabric scraps cut into circles or squares, or cotton balls. You will also need thread or yarn, drinking straws cut into segments, and a large plastic darning needle.
- Thread the needle and tie one end to an egg carton section and the other end to the needle. Begin adding materials, like colorful circles separated by straw segments and egg cups, until the yarn is full. You may need adult help to poke holes in the egg carton cups and paper circles in advance.
- Tie another piece of yarn to this, and keep on going. There is no right or wrong way to assemble the pieces, but it does help to space the little straw segments evenly between larger pieces to keep the items separated. Some artists like to make a garland to drape around a window or room rather than a necklace or lei. It just takes more materials and supplies and time.

DAY 3

Mooshed Carton Pulp

- Squeeze out the water from the pulp. Further pull and tear the pulpy paper to break up all the fibers. Then mix and knead in an adhesive like glue or paste. White glue is handy and works fine; wallpaper paste also works.
  Note: Do not use liquid starch; it will not work.
- When well-mixed, place the pulp in a plastic bowl. Now the pulp is ready to use to form little sculptures, objects, odd shapes, or ornaments. Let the objects air-dry on waxed paper.
- When dry, color the pulp objects with acrylic paints or markers.

> **A note on egg carton safety:** According to the Center for Disease Control, there has never been a documented case of salmonella contracted from an egg carton craft. However, we must consider that egg cartons hold a remote possibility of salmonella bacteria from cracked or leaking eggs. Though research shows the possibility is extremely small, please make your own decision when choosing to use egg cartons. Heat destroys salmonella: You may choose to wash Styrofoam egg cartons in very hot soapy water, or heat cardboard cartons in a 350°F oven for 10–15 minutes (watch closely). As an alternative, you can also buy unused clean cartons from a craft store.

DAY 4

One Dozen Chickies Craft

- Glue a drawing on the outside cover and inside cover of a clean, empty egg carton to hide the pictures and print on the egg carton.
- Glue a little tuft of Easter grass inside each cup.
- To make the chicky, glue a cotton ball on the Easter grass in each cup. (Some cosmetic cotton balls come in yellow and pink, which are great colors for this activity.)
- To make a face on the chicky, glue little scraps of construction paper eyes and beaks on the cotton ball. Twelve little chickies all tucked into their carton nest! Keep the chickies in the carton, or add them to other decorations.
- *Chickies One-by-One Idea:* Cut the egg carton apart into 12 individual cups, and decorate just one chicky per cup. Each chicky will look like it just hatched from an egg!

DAY 5

Bumpy Canvas Painting

- Step up the artistic process a few notches and make something extremely creative!
- Place a large "egg flat" on a flat workspace. An egg flat is like a very big egg carton that has no lid, and is usually blue, gray, or beige in color. (If you do not have an egg flat, cut four or six paper egg cartons apart, and glue or staple the bumpy rectangle sections together side by side to form a larger carton surface.)
- Completely cover the outside of the bumpy carton with one color of tempera paint (the part the eggs sit in is face down and not painted). Dry briefly.
- With the painted side facing up, paint a picture or design with tempera paints. The carton bumps make this "canvas" an artistic challenge, which ultimately yields a visually captivating painting.
  Note: Some artists prefer to paint designs and patterns as a first exploration on the "bumpy canvas," while other artists will jump in and paint a detailed picture.
- *Frame Idea:* When the "bumpy canvas" is dry, create a silver frame for it by adding duct tape around the outside edge of the carton to bind the edges.

Egg Cartons

Fabric Scraps

Cut some fabric scraps in squares, snip some into strips, and fringe or fray others for this week's art fun.

Materials for Day 1 | fabric scraps cut into 1"–2" squares (many colors, patterns, and textures) • scissors • square of heavy paper tacky glue (Sobo®, Tacky Glue®)

Materials for Day 2 | fabric to cover a heavy piece of cardboard • masking tape or duct tape • ribbon or yarn • optional—objects to tuck into the board: photos, drawings, collage items • materials for decorating the board (see Day 2 for ideas)

Materials for Day 3 | plain fabric • scissors • kitchen sponges to cut into shapes • waxed paper • masking tape • fabric paints poured on well-washed plastic or vegetable trays from the grocery store, or paper plates • a way to display (see Day 3 for ideas) • something more to decorate (see Day 3 for ideas)

Materials for Day 4 | plain white T-shirt • fabric crayons • white paper • ironing board (or protected table) and iron—adult only • old towels

Materials for Day 5 | workspace covered with cardboard or several layers of newspaper • white fabric • tape • white glue in squeeze bottle • adult: rubber gloves • fabric craft dye (choose one color or several colors) • hand-sprayer • cold water • to display, choose from: cardboard and tape, wire and clothespins, wall, or bulletin board

DAY 1

Fabric Squares Collage

- Cut fabric scraps into 1"–2" squares. Glue the squares on a heavy square of paper with tacky glue (fabric glue).
  Note: White glue also works, but a glue stick will not work.
- Glue squares in any pattern of choice. Some pattern ideas include overlapping the squares randomly; placing the squares edge to edge, alternating colors; creating quilt-like patterns; alternating fuzzy and smooth patterns; and so on.
- Let the fabric collage dry completely.

DAY 2

Fabric & Ribbon Design Board

- Cover a thick piece of cardboard (a square between 6"–12" works best) with a piece of fabric. The fabric can be patterned or plain, textured or smooth; any choice is fine.
- Wrap the fabric edges around to the back side of the cardboard and secure with masking tape, making sure the fabric is smooth and tight across the front of the cardboard.
- Wrap ribbon (or yarn) around the covered cardboard in a pattern to create a crisscross design of any kind. Tie or tape the ribbon tightly on the back of the cardboard.
- The art is now complete; however, if you want to add more, try these ideas:
  - ○ Tuck small photos into the ribbon areas.
  - ○ Tuck collage items, like cotton balls or feathers, between the ribbons.
  - ○ Glue decorative items to the fabric or ribbons, like buttons, beads, paper dots, or sequins.
  - ○ Add designs with puffy fabric paint or glitter glue.

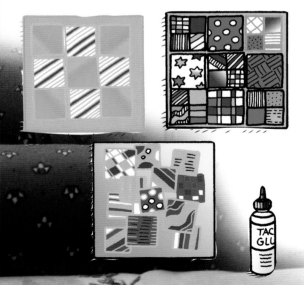

Printing on Fabric

- Cut common kitchen sponges into simple shapes, like squares, circles, or triangles. A heart, star, cloud, or tulip will also work.
- Spread a piece of plain fabric on waxed paper on your workspace. (The waxed paper will protect the space.) Tape the waxed paper to the work surface and use more tape to hold the fabric to the waxed paper so it will not wrinkle or wiggle as you work.
- Pour puddles of fabric paints onto plastic grocery trays or paper plates. Press slightly damp sponge shapes into paint, and then test them on scrap paper. When satisfied, press the sponge with paint onto the fabric, making a print. To preserve color clarity, rinse and squeeze the sponges between colors if you are using several colors. Allow the fabric and paint to dry overnight.
- On the next day, remove the tape and display the design by hanging squares of decorated fabric from a "clothesline" with clothespins, or pin them to a bulletin board or blank wall.
- *Customized Fabric Idea:* Decorate an apron, plain cloth napkins, a tablecloth, pillowcase, or other plain fabric items with fabric paint sponge prints.

T-Shirt Transfer Craft

- Find a plain white cotton or poly-cotton T-shirt. Create a design for the T-shirt by drawing the design with fabric crayons on any white paper. **Note:** Fabric crayons are usually available at any store that has school supplies or regular crayons, and at all craft stores.
- Color firmly and fill in the design with lots of color. The colors will look dull, but will become bright and beautiful when ironed.
- To transfer the design, spread the T-shirt on an ironing board or table (protect the table with a pad of towels). Turn the drawing face-down on the T-shirt. Ask an adult to press firmly with a warm iron, following the directions on the fabric crayon box. Do not use steam. Press firmly for about 30 seconds to transfer the crayon to the shirt. Try not to peek! Peel off the paper, and see the bright and clear transfer. This design will wash and dry beautifully for years! **Note:** If you are writing a word or name, write it backwards on the paper so it will transfer correctly to the T-shirt.

Glue Batik

- Protect your workspace with cardboard or several layers of newspaper. Tape a piece of white fabric to the covered table.
- Squeeze a thick design of white glue on the white fabric. The places with glue will remain uncolored or white. Use thick glue lines where pure white is preferred. Then let dry.
- Meanwhile, ask an adult to put on rubber gloves, mix fabric craft dye according to package directions, and then pour the dye into spray bottles. One color is enough, although you may want to use several colors.
- Spray the fabric with color. Be sure the work area is prepared for over-spray, or work outdoors on the grass. When satisfied with the sprayed color, let the fabric dry indoors overnight on clean newspapers or cardboard.
- The next day, rinse the fabric in cold water just long enough to remove the glue. Don't be surprised when some color also rinses away. Let the fabric dry once again.
- To display, attach the dry batik to a bulletin board or a piece of cardboard. Fabric batik could cover a square of cardboard with the edges taped to the back. For easy display, hang fabric squares from a wire with clothespins.

Gift Wrap

Gift wrap comes in many wonderful patterns and colors, from floral to foil, with snowmen or balloons, bright colors or pastels. The variety is inspiring! Save pieces of used paper from birthday parties or holiday gifts for art explorations.

Materials for Day 1 | wrapping paper (gift wrap), recycled or new • drawing paper or construction paper • markers or crayons • scissors • white glue or glue stick

Materials for Day 2 | wrapping paper (gift wrap), recycled or new • white drawing paper • markers or crayons • scissors • yarn or wiggly eyes • white glue

Materials for Day 3 | sheets of wrapping paper (gift wrap), recycled or new • pencil • clear tape • scissors • optional—cardboard base • optional—decorating materials like ribbons or stickers

Materials for Day 4 | wrapping paper (gift wrap), recycled or new • used greeting card or note card • scissors • thinned white glue and a brush • white paper • crayons or markers • pencil, pen, or marker

Materials for Day 5 | small boxes—choose from: gift boxes, jewelry boxes, shoeboxes, containers, cartons • scissors • glue and tape • ribbons

DAY 1

Scrap Wrap Collage

- Draw a large, simple shape on drawing paper or construction paper. Some ideas for the shape include a flower, fish, boat, or simply a square or circle. Simple shapes work best.
- Cut or tear scraps of leftover gift wrap into pieces to fill the shape with color and patterns. Glue the paper shapes into the collage.
- Use strips or squares of gift wrap to glue a paper frame around the finished collage.

DAY 2

Dress-Up Paper Person

- Draw the shape of a person on drawing paper. Use gift wrap scraps to cut out clothing for the paper person to wear. Some ideas include drawing a dress, pants, shirt, coat, hat, socks, pajamas, or shoes.
- Glue the clothing to the person. Complete the design with markers to make a face, hair, hands, or other features. Consider adding yarn or wiggly eyes for hair and eyes.

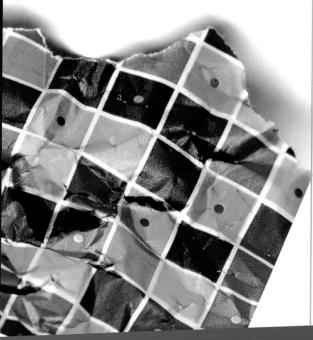

Paper Roll Sculpture

- Cut gift wrap into about 12" squares. Cut at least 10 squares; more will be even better.
- To make rolls, start at the corner of a square on the "wrong side" of the paper, and place a pencil across the point diagonally. Roll the paper around the pencil all the way across the square. Then hold the roll and gently let the pencil fall out. Tape the roll at the center to ensure it will hold. Make at least 10 gift-wrap paper tubes. The more, the better! Snip off the ends of the tubes to keep them tidy, or leave them as they are.
- Use clear tape to begin taping the colorful tubes together in any design, random or planned, creating a sculpture that grows. Tape the tubes to a cardboard base, or simply tape them together in a variety of ways. You can also bend the tubes, join them end to end, or slip one tube inside another to create extra long tubes.
- Experiment and explore how to join the tubes in various ways to build a colorful sculpture. Consider adding other art supplies to the sculpture, like colorful ribbons or stickers.

Homemade Gift Wrap Greeting Card

- Select a used greeting card. It can open from the top or from the side. Open the card and place it face up on your work surface.
- Choose a favorite piece of wrapping paper and cut a piece to fit on the front of the folded card.
- Use a brush to paint the front of the card with white glue thinned with water. Press the gift wrap onto the glue. Trim away any paper extending beyond the edges of the card. Cover any writing inside the card with a piece of white or colored paper.
- Create a drawing or design on a piece of plain paper at least 1" smaller all around than the size of the card. Glue this on the front of the card, allowing the gift wrap to frame the design.
- Write a special message inside the card, and give the card to someone special. Don't forget to sign your name!

Wrapped Gift Box Assemblage

- Gather small boxes, cartons, and containers of all kinds. Wrap each one as a gift with a variety of wrapping papers, tape, and ribbons.
- Arrange and stack the wrapped boxes together in a satisfying assemblage. Use glue and tape to attach the gifts in a permanent sculpture display of stacked and assembled wrapped "gifts."

Gift Wrap

Greeting Cards

Old greeting cards are treasures for recycling into new customized art cards or cut-and-paste artworks.

Materials for Day 1 | used greeting cards • cardstock or heavy paper or purchased blank note cards • scissors • glue or tape • crayons or markers • white paper • pen or pencil

Materials for Day 2 | used greeting cards • white paper • stapler • scissors • glue or tape • pencil or pen

Materials for Day 3 | used greeting cards • scissors • construction paper • white glue or glue stick

Materials for Day 4 | used greeting cards with a blank reverse side • scissors, craft scissors with shape edges, pinking shears • markers • hole punch • choice of ribbon, string, twine, raffia, yarn

Materials for Day 5 | used greeting cards • scissors • box lid • glue or tape • drawing paper • crayons or markers • optional— decorate the box lid: tempera paint and brushes, colored paper and glue

DAY 1

"New from Old" Cards

- Use a rectangle of cardstock folded in half, or purchased blank note cards, to create new, personalized, and customized greeting cards. Cut an image from a used greeting card and glue it to a new blank card. In this way, you can make many new cards to give throughout the year for birthdays, holidays, thank-you notes, "just because" occasions, or other special times.
- Use your imagination to redesign the new cards, using crayons or markers to enhance the design.
- Make homemade envelopes by folding a sheet of white paper in half, gluing the two open sides, and leaving the top open.
- When ready to use, slip the new card inside, fold the top over, and glue the top edge to seal in the card. Address, stamp, and mail, or deliver in person.
- *Messages Idea:* Write messages inside the new cards, or cut a printed message from a used card and glue it into the new card. Don't forget to sign your name!

DAY 2

Little Book

- To make a little individual book, fold and staple 4 or 5 sheets of blank paper to create a book with a total of 8 to 10 pages, counting both sides.
- Glue interesting pictures or images from used greeting cards on the blank pages.
- Dictate to an adult or write sentences or stories about each page, or print words or letters by hand.
- Turn the pages of the little book and read aloud. Counting and alphabet books are especially fun to make.

Slip & Slide Optical Cut-Up

- Choose a greeting card with an eye-catching art image or design that covers the entire front of the card from edge to edge. Cut on the fold to separate the front page of the card from the rest. You will be using only the front page of the card for this activity. Cut the front piece into straight strips, wiggly strips, or squares. It is best to limit the number of pieces to no more than 20 (6–12 is a good workable number; 3 would be a minimum).
- Assemble all of the pieces back together, like a puzzle, on a sheet of colored paper. Now "slip and slide" the pieces apart slightly, and then a little more, so you see spaces between the pieces.
- Glue the pieces on the colored paper with the spaces showing. Let the glue dry. The artwork will have the attributes of an optical illusion, and will be visually interesting.
- *Picture Mix-Up Idea:* Glue the pieces on the colored paper "out of order," rather than fitting them together like a puzzle. You may need a larger piece of paper to accommodate the random assembling of pieces, depending on how you overlap and spread them out.

Gift Tag Craft

- Used greeting cards make unique gift tags for holidays, birthdays, and special occasions. Choose cards that are blank on the reverse side, with nothing written on the back of the picture.
- Choose the part of the picture you like. Cut around it in any shape, such as a square, circle, heart, tree, star, or any shape you like. Lines may be straight, wavy, or extra fancy. Craft scissors or pinking shears will add a designer edge to the tag.
  - With a marker, write "To: _____" and "From: _____" on the back of the tag. Other messages may be added depending on the occasion, like, "Happy Birthday, Michael" or "I love my mom!"
  - Punch a hole. Attach the tag to a gift with your choice of ribbon or yarn.
- **Note:** Gifts do not need to be wrapped to be special. A jar of homemade jam with a creative tag will look festive and personalized. A baggie filled with homemade playdough will be a great gift for a friend's birthday; add the tag and the gift is ready to give!

Stand-Ups

- Cut out people, objects, animals, and other interesting things from used greeting cards. Leave extra paper on the bottom edge of each one to make "tabs." Large tabs give the most stability.
- Fold the tabs back. Glue the tabs into the lid of a box to make the pieces stand up—a "stand-up" artwork. This artwork can tell a story, create a scene, or just be interesting to view, like a 3-D collage.
- Draw other objects or people and cut them out, leaving tabs on the bottom edges, and add these to the work.
  Note: Consider lining the box lid with colored paper or painting it before adding Stand-Ups. If you want to paint the box lid, do this the day before so the lid has time to dry completely and the glue or tape will hold the Stand-Ups.

Brown paper bags (lunch-sized bags to full-sized grocery bags) are very useful for art, whether disassembled and cut apart or used intact.

Materials for Day 1 | brown paper grocery bag • scissors • colored chalk or pastels • cosmetic pad or facial tissue • optional—iron or ironing board or padded surface (adult use only)

Materials for Day 2 | brown paper grocery bag • drawing paper • tempera paints in cups • ping-pong ball in each cup • plastic spoon for each cup • newsprint or tray • water for rinsing • wet rags or paper towels

Materials for Day 3 | grocery bags, lunch bags, any brown paper bags • scissors • pencil with eraser • paint in shallow dish or tray (liquid watercolors or tempera paints) • optional, for display: cardboard and tape • optional, for gift tag: yarn, pencil or pen, scrap of plain brown paper

Materials for Day 4 | large paper grocery bags • scissors • collage materials (see Day 4 for ideas) • stapler, tape, white glue

Materials for Day 5 | any size brown paper bag • chalk, tempera paint and paintbrushes, crayons, markers • magazine pictures of faces • scissors • decorating materials—choose from a combination of: chalk, fabric scraps, ribbon, junk jewelry • pencil • filler materials (see Day 5 for ideas)

DAY 1

Price-Saver Chalk Art

- Cut away the bottom of a brown paper bag. Then cut one side seam to open the bag. Flatten the bag on your workspace. Trim the edges of the bag if they are ragged. (If desired, ask an adult to iron the paper bag very flat with an iron set on medium and no steam.)
- Turn the bag over to the blank side. With colored chalk (pastel chalk, sidewalk chalk, chalkboard chalk, or any chalk), draw on the brown paper. Chalk will adhere nicely to the rough paper and colors will show up well.
  Note: Chalk is inherently smudgy and easily transfers to clothes and skin, so plan accordingly.
- *Brushed Chalk Idea:* Take a facial tissue or cosmetic pad and brush and blend the chalk lines for more art exploration and design.

DAY 2

Shake-It-Up Bag Painting

Note: Have wet rags or paper towels on hand to wipe your hands during this art experience.
- Place a sheet of drawing paper in a bag. Either roll it like a tube and insert it in the bag, or cut it to fit the bottom of the bag. The way you place the paper in the bag will change your paint design results, so enjoy experimenting.
- Fill a few cups with your choice of tempera paint colors. Place a ping-pong ball in each cup, rolling it over and over with a plastic spoon to coat. Use the spoon to drop all the ping-pong balls into the bag.
- Roll the top of the bag over several times to close it and to give you a hand-hold. Shake the bag vigorously or gently; shake it any way you want for as long as you want!
- Open the bag. Pour the ping-pong balls out on a sheet of newsprint or a tray to rinse and then reuse. Carefully reach into the bag and remove the paper to see the Shake-It-Up paint design.

DAY 3

Eraser Dots

- To make a uniquely designed artwork, flatten a paper bag the same way as on Day 1. Dip or press the eraser of a pencil in a shallow dish of paint, liquid watercolor, or on a stamp pad, and then make dot prints on the paper bag. Cover the entire bag with dots.
- Decide how to decorate the dots with markers. Dots can become flowers, noses on animals, fish eyes, ladybugs, apples, and so on.
- Another creative idea is to decorate and make designs around the dots with squiggles, lines, or swirls.
- *Display Idea:* Tape the edges of the bag over a piece of cardboard to make it easy to display.
- *Gift Wrap and Tag Idea:* Use the hand-designed paper to wrap a special gift. Add a brown paper scrap for a "to and from" tag and attach it with yarn or tape.

DAY 4

Big Fancy Hat Craft

- Roll down the top edge of a large paper grocery bag, rolling it several times. Try on the bag as a big hat. Does it fit? If not, pinch the bag smaller to fit, and ask an adult to staple or tape the paper bag to fit tighter.
- Decorate all sides of the hat using crayons or markers. Glue on any collage materials like ribbon, feathers, paper scraps, yarn, buttons, glitter, cotton balls, paper or silk flowers, and so on. Some artists like to pull their hats down over their eyes and ask an adult to help them cut eye-holes through which they can peek through the hat.

DAY 5

Brown Bag Beastie

- Create a brown bag funny-face "beastie" to place in a window, on a shelf, or anywhere a funny face will be enjoyed. Begin by placing a brown bag (grocery or lunch-size, large or small) folded flat on your workspace in its natural form, with the folded end toward you. No need to cut it apart.
- Cut facial features from magazine pictures and glue them to the bag to form a funny beastie face. Use other materials to add features. Some ideas include using chalk to add color to cheeks or nose, adding fabric scraps to make hair bows or collars, ribbon for hair decoration, and adding old earrings for jewelry. Let the collage pieces inspire you.
- To create a funny hairdo for the beastie, cut the open (top) edge of the bag in points, zigzags, fringes, rounded, or any way desired. Curl the paper strips around a pencil, or fringe and crop them further to add character. Open the beastie bag and stand it up. To keep the beastie from blowing away, place a, brick, wood scrap, or rock in the bag to keep it in place for display.
- *Fill the Beastie Idea:* To give the beastie even more character, fill the bag with something interesting that will poke from the open top, like dried twigs, shredded paper, or balls of newspaper.

Hole-Punch Dots

Offices and schools are great places to collect a box of hole-punch dots, usually in an array of colors.

Materials for Day 1 | paper-punch dots (paper circles from hole punch) • shapes • white glue (in a squeeze bottle, or in a cup with a paintbrush) • construction paper • optional—decorating materials: crayons, markers, any chosen collage items

Materials for Day 2 | paper-punch dots, craft hole-punch shapes • white glue (in a squeeze bottle or in a cup with a paintbrush) • construction paper, drawing paper, tagboard or poster board • crayons, markers, or colored pencils • optional— cotton swab

Materials for Day 3 | strip of tagboard • hand-held single-hole punch, craft punch, or scrapbooking punches • tempera paint in a shallow tray (several colors) Note: liquid watercolors will also work well • sponge or paintbrush • white drawing paper

Materials for Day 4 | paper-punch dots • construction paper • scissors • larger sheet of paper for mural • white glue or glue stick • crayons or markers • optional—hand-held sprayer filled with thin blue paint

Materials for Day 5 | heavy paper plate or poster board square • hand-held single-hole punch • paper-punch dots • yarn in different colors • masking tape • scissors • white glue

DAY 1

Easy Sprinkle

- Squeeze lines of glue on colored paper from a bottle of glue. Painting glue lines on paper with a brush is another technique that works well.
- Sprinkle hole-punch dots on the glue lines, much like the technique of sprinkling glitter on glue. Shake the ones that do not stick back onto a tray or into a container. Add more dots at this time if you wish. Then allow the dot art to dry.
- Consider filling in more of the design with markers, crayons, or collage items.
  Hint: Make your own dots with a hand-held paper punch and any kind of paper, including the Sunday comics, colorful magazine pages, wrapping paper, construction paper, colored paper, or junk mail. You can use a hand-held single-hole punch, a craft punch, or scrapbooking punches. A three-hole punch device for three-ring binders will produce dots in a jiffy.
  Note: You will need multiple hole-punch dots for Days 1, 2, and 4.

DAY 2

Color Fill

- Save hole-punch paper dots, or make paper dots from colored paper scraps to get just the colors desired. (Save the scraps with holes for Day 3: Hole-Punch Stencil.)
- Draw a simple picture or design on a piece of paper with bold shapes or sections (details won't work as well). Fill in the sections either of the following two ways:
  - Carefully attach dots with glue, placing one dot at a time, in parts of the picture that need to be filled with color (use a toothpick dipped in glue to pick up and place dots).
  - Sprinkle lots of dots over lots of glue spread in the spaces that need to be filled. Shake loose dots onto a tray or sheet of newspaper to be reused.
- Either way is effective for filling in the design with colorful dots. Dry the filled art design.
- *Paint Dots Idea:* Dip a cotton swab in paint to add more colorful dots with a different look.
- *Shape Punches Idea:* Save shaped punches from craft punches. For example, snowflake punches can help create a wild snowstorm artwork!

Hole-Punch Stencil

- Fill a strip of tagboard with punch holes, or use the scraps left from the Color Fill activity on Day 2.
- Place the paper with holes over a sheet of drawing paper. Tape it down gently at the corners. Dab a sponge or paintbrush full of paint over the dots, trying not to wiggle the punched paper.
- Lift and remove the paper. Colorful painted dots will be left on the paper. Continue changing colors and making a design with various stencil shapes and punched holes.

Tropical Fish Craft

- Cut out unusual tropical fish shapes from colorful construction paper. Decorate each fish in a different way, gluing on hole-punch dots for eyes and scales, and using markers or crayons to add decorations and features.
- Glue all the fish on one larger sheet of paper, like they are swimming in a colorful school. Add bubbles with more punch dots. For an extra-"oceany" look, use a hand-held sprayer to lightly spray the entire fish art with a fine mist of thin blue paint. Have extra newspaper on hand to protect the table or floor when using the spray technique. Allow the artwork to dry briefly before handling.

Yarn Weave

- Punch holes all around the outside edge of a sturdy paper plate or poster board square, as far in as the punch will reach. Set aside the dots until later.
- Cut colorful yarn strands into manageable lengths, about 24" long or less. Wrap a piece of masking tape around the end of a strand of yarn to make a quick "sewing needle."
- Pull the full length of the yarn up through one hole and across the paper plate or poster board. Tape the loose end of the yarn onto the back to secure it. Push the yarn "needle" down through another hole. Continue weaving and lacing the yarn in and out of the holes, changing colors whenever desired. Tape stray ends of yarn down on the back of the plate or poster board square. Running the yarn through a hole more than once will add to the thickness and color of the weaving.
- When satisfied with the yarn design, glue dots here and there in the blank spaces or even directly on yarn strands. Dry completely.

Hole-Punch Dots

Jars

Jelly, mayonnaise, peanut butter, pickles, relish, marshmallow fluff, and honey—it is beginning to sound like an art picnic! Wash and dry empty plastic jars and lids well, and enjoy a week of art activities that are useful as well as absolutely unique.

Materials for Day 1 | wide-mouth plastic jar • Plasticine® modeling clay in bright colors (also called playclay) • optional—Fimo® or Sculpey®

Materials for Day 2 | small empty squeeze bottles • white glue mixed with liquid watercolors • baby food jars with lids • optional—glitter

Materials for Day 3 | large empty plastic jar with lid • photograph • colored paper • scissors • glue and tape • stuffing materials (see Day 3 for ideas) • optional—sequins, paper scraps, glitter

Materials for Day 4 | tall, clear plastic bottle or plastic jar • shredded white paper • pencil with eraser • black permanent marker • snowman materials (see Day 4 for ideas) • scissors • white glue in squeeze bottle

Materials for Day 5 | small clear plastic jar with lid • layering materials (see Day 5 for ideas) • paper cup for pouring • chopstick • tape

DAY 1

Playclay Inside-Out Jar

- Wide-mouth jars (with or without lids) work best for this popular art activity.
  Note: An adult should make sure the jar is large enough for a child's hand to fit easily inside the opening.
- Select several colors of Plasticine® modeling clay, the colorful soft clay that does not dry out (available in any store with art materials). Other kinds of colored playclay work too, but Plasticine® is easiest to smear and mix.
- Pinch a small blob from a stick or block of Plasticine® playclay, and press the soft colored clay inside the jar, smearing it with your fingers to cover a small area with a thin layer. Add another pinch of a different color, and do the same, letting the two colors join and mix. Continue until the inside of the jar is completely covered with colorful smears and swirls. Watching the colors mix from the outside of the jar as you smear them on the inside is inspiring!
- Place in a sunny window to see the colors light up.
- *Picture Clay Idea:* Some adept artists like to make pictures with the playclay by pressing parts of the design in a definite order.

Note: With supervision, older children can use glass jars.

DAY 2

Swirly Glue Baby Food Jars

- Make colored glue by mixing white glue with liquid watercolors (or a little tempera paint or food coloring). Then fill small squeeze bottles with colored glue. (Pre-colored glue comes ready to use in small squeeze bottles.) If no squeeze bottles are handy, use medium paintbrushes and cups of colored glue.
- Squeeze or drop colored glue onto the insides of a small baby-food jar. Use enough glue that it is dripping and sliding around. Consider adding a little glitter glue. Screw the lid on tightly.
- Experiment with different ways to make the colors swirl together: roll the jar slowly on the table or between your hands, shake the jar, rotate the jar in the air, or move the glue around inside the jar in some way until the entire jar is coated with swirls. Then let the jar sit undisturbed and dry several days. The glue will dry hard and shiny with a stained-glass look.

Glittery Photo Jar

- Fill the bottom of a large, clean mayonnaise or peanut butter jar with a soft material, like fluffed cotton, shredded paper, shredded foil, feathers, tinsel, or Easter grass.
- Glue a favorite photograph to a piece of colored paper or poster board to make it stiff. Bend it slightly and slide it into the jar, "planting" it in the soft lining. (You can glue a photo on both sides of the colored paper if you wish.)
- Add glittery or fluffy items to the jar, like shredded foil, bits of foil wrapping paper, feathers, or tinsel. You can also glue sequins to the inside wall of the jar with just a small dot of glue. Make sure you can still see the photo.
- If the jar has a lid, tape curled pieces of foil paper or lengths of tinsel to the lid so they can hang into the jar but do not hide the photo. Put the lid on the jar. Then cover the lid with aluminum foil and more collage materials. If there is no lid, consider decorating the opening edge of the jar with silver duct tape, sewing trim, glitter and glue, or glittery paper.
- Paint a bit of glue on the jar here and there, including the opening, and roll in glitter for a final glittery effect.
  Hint: Instead of a photo, you can use an original drawing or small painting.

Snowman Craft Jar

- To make a snowman jar, cut or tear used white paper into small pieces and stuff a bottle or tall jar with the scraps until the jar is full.
  Hint: Use the eraser end of a pencil to push the paper deep into the jar, until the jar looks white. (Mixed colors of paper are fun too!)
- To make a snowman hat, color the jar lid with black permanent marker. Then glue a black film canister to the lid. Consider tying ribbon or felt around the hat. To make eyes, glue dots of black paper or small black pompoms onto the jar. Eyes could be drawn with permanent black marker too. Glue a button nose on the snowman, or make a carrot with a small triangle of orange felt. Glue several more buttons or pompoms on the jar-body of the snowman. Wrap ribbon or felt around the jar to resemble a scarf.
- The snowman is now complete; however, you can still add any number of other features. For example, cut soda straws and tape them to the snowman for arms. Cut mittens from felt and glue to the arms. Add glitter glue for sparkle.
- Feeling inspired? Create another character instead of a snowman! Make a snow woman, snow child, bunny, leprechaun, elf, boy or girl, dog, cat, or any imaginary creature.

Make Layers!

- Traditionally, most layered jars are made with colored sand that you pour into a clear jar, which shows off the layered designs. Think about adding something new to the layers (with or without the sand). Work with one material, or combine several for this exploration and experiment!
- Begin with a small clear jar, and consider using any of the following materials for layering: natural or colored sand, aquarium gravel or pebbles, confetti or tiny paper bits, colored playclay or playdough, glitter or sequins.
- To layer pourable materials, place the material in a paper cup and pinch the rim of the cup to form a spout. Pour some of the material carefully into the jar. Use your hands to place non-pourable materials in the jar. Continue to add layers.
- Try pushing some of the materials with a chopstick to change the way the layering looks. Also try tipping the jar a little to one side to get a slanted layer.
- Layer the materials until the jar is full to the top. It is a good idea to tape the lid on the jar when it is full. Try not to shake the jar once you complete the layering.

Junk Mail

Junk mail holds treasures for creating art! There may be gold hidden inside! Gold paper, that is.

Materials for Day 1 | shredded junk mail: flyers, envelopes, advertisements, mailers, booklets, and so on • drawing paper, butcher paper, gift bags, paper bags, other various papers • crayons, markers, scissors • glue, tape, stapler

Materials for Day 2 | strips of paper made from junk mail • pencil for curling paper • scissors • tape, glue, stapler • base for art (see Day 2 for ideas)

Materials for Day 3 | newspaper, newsprint, or butcher paper for the artwork • crayons, markers, or colored pencils • scissors • tape, glue, stapler, decorating materials (see Day 3 for ideas) • junk mail or shredded paper for stuffing the art • yarn

Materials for Day 4 | glossy coated junk mail • scissors • toothpick, pencil • white glue • kite string or dental floss • optional—additional beads from broken jewelry, plastic craft beads, beads made from dough or clay • plastic needle for threading beads

Materials for Day 5 | colorful junk mail • scissors • white glue or glue stick • construction paper, 2 sheets in contrasting colors

DAY 1

Shredded Paper Creation Station

- Ask an adult to shred junk mail through a paper shredder to make a bag full of fluffy shreds. If shredded paper is not available, snip mail into thin strips and pieces and collect the pieces in a bag or box. Use shredded junk mail to:
  - Create artwork using glue, tape, paper, markers, and other materials.
  - Make collages on cardboard or paper.
  - Embellish artwork with 3-D hair, clouds, snow, or smoke.
  - Stuff artwork (see Day 3, Puffed Art).
  - Fill gift bags or other crafts needing attractive fill.

DAY 2

Curly Mail

- Tear or cut colorful junk mail into a pile of strips ½"–2" wide. Roll a strip tightly around a pencil, release, and set aside. The paper strip will be curled. Turn the pile of strips into a pile of curls!
- Part of the fun of Curly Mail is choosing a background paper or object. Some ideas include using construction paper cut into a shape like a circle, square, or triangle; a paper party plate; a cylinder roll of colored paper (tape to hold); an oatmeal box; a soup can covered with gift wrap or more junk mail; and so on.
- Staple, tape, or glue curls of paper all over the background paper or object until it is completely covered with curls.

DAY 3

Puffed Art

- Place two sheets of newspaper, newsprint, or butcher paper on your work surface, one on top of the other. Draw a large, simple shape to fill the paper from edge to edge. Some ideas include drawing a fish, flower, heart, cloud, happy face, sun, cat, or a geometric shape.
- Cut out the shape, cutting through both sheets of paper at once to get two identical pieces.
- Keeping the edges lined up, staple all around the double sheets leaving a 6"–12" opening on one side.
- Decorate the shape with tempera paints, or glue on scrap paper, streamers, or crepe paper. When the shape is dry enough for you to handle, stuff it with junk mail scrunched into balls, so the shape puffs up. Consider using shredded paper from Day 1 to fill the shape. It will take a lot of junk mail to fill the Puffed Art!
- When the Puffed Art is full, close the opening with staples. Hang the Puffed Art from yarn tied through holes or stapled to the top of the shape.

DAY 4

Junk Mail Jewelry Craft

- Cut glossy or coated junk mail into small strips about 1" x 4". To make a bead, roll a strip by wrapping it around a toothpick starting with a short end. Glue the last ½" of paper to the roll to create the bead, and then remove the toothpick. (Make larger beads from longer strips of paper wrapped around a pencil.) Repeat until there are enough beads to fill a string for a necklace that fits over your head.
- String the beads on strong string, like kite string or dental floss. First measure the string so it is long enough to go over your head easily, with extra length for tying. Some artists like to add beads from broken necklaces or bracelets between their junk mail beads or beads made from dough or clay; others prefer stringing only junk mail beads.
- When the string is full, tie a knot to complete the necklace. Slip the necklace over your head and wear it proudly.

DAY 5

Stencil over Strips

- Cut colorful junk mail into strips ¼"–1" wide. Glue the strips in rows on a colorful piece of paper (or on a background of more junk mail), leaving spaces between the strips.
- As the glue dries, choose a second sheet of paper in a contrasting color. Cut large holes from the paper with cutout spaces and uncut spaces (like a stencil or a paper snowflake).
- Place the second paper with holes over the first paper with strips so you can see the rows through the holes. Glue the sheet with holes in place and then let it dry.
- *Cut-and-Paste Idea:* As a creative alternative, consider cutting mail into shapes other than strips and arrange them in ways other than rows.

Leaves

Collect lovely leaves, fresh green or colorful, supple autumn varieties for a week of leaf art!

Materials for Day 1 | leaf—choose a fresh green one or a supple autumn leaf • watercolor paints and paintbrush • drawing paper or construction paper • optional—tempera paint mixed with liquid starch, and a paintbrush; colored paper or fabric

Materials for Day 2 | leaves (If real leaves are not available, use heavy paper cut into leaf shapes) • drawing paper • damp sponge • thin tempera paint or liquid watercolors in a shallow tray

Materials for Day 3 | watercolor paint and paintbrush • drawing paper • leaves • optional—fine or medium point marker

Materials for Day 4 | 2 or 3 fresh green or supple autumn leaves or paper leaves • large drawing paper • black marker (permanent markers work best) • crayons, colored pencils, and markers

Materials for Day 5 | one large leaf, either a real leaf or one cut from paper • electric buffet warming tray—adult supervision needed • mittens or work gloves to protect hands • old, peeled stubs of crayon • stick or thin tree branch from outdoors (12"–18" long), or a paper towel tube • string, thread, or yarn • paper towels or rag for clean up

DAY 1

Basic Leaf Paint & Print

- Place a leaf on a covered workspace. Paint the leaf with watercolor paints. While the leaf is still wet, press white paper on the painted leaf, patting and pressing with your fingers to help the paper pick up the paint design.
- Lift the paper from the leaf to see the print transferred to the white paper.
  Hint: Sometimes the leaf sticks to the paper and needs to be peeled away.
- *Tempera Paint Idea:* Hold a leaf on a covered workspace with one hand. With the other hand, brush tempera paint mixed with liquid starch on the leaf (the colors will be bright and glossy). Next, press a sheet of paper on the leaf and rub the paper gently to absorb the print. Lift the paper to see the print made by the leaf on the paper. Make more prints! Try colored paper or fabric to see leaf prints in new ways.

Hint: If real leaves are not available use artificial leaves or leaves cut from paper.

DAY 2

Leaf Burst

- Choose whole, complete leaves with good edges, either fresh green leaves or supple fall leaves. If leaves are unavailable, draw bold leaf shapes on paper and cut them out to use instead.
- Hold a leaf firmly on a sheet of drawing paper with one hand. Dip a damp sponge into thin paint with the other hand. Dab all around the edges of the leaf, brushing the sponge outward from the leaf's edge onto the paper creating a "burst" design.
- Gently lift the leaf from the paper to see the clean stencil with a brushed burst design. Make several bursts on one paper, changing colors and overlapping shapes, if desired.

Watercolor Leaf Paint

- Cover a sheet of drawing paper with very wet watercolor paints. Paint color all over the paper without making a picture. Press leaves into the paint in any pattern or arrangement.
- Let the painting dry completely, usually overnight.
- Peel off the leaves and see the design images remaining in the paint.
- *Art Leaves Idea:* Paint leaf shapes on drawing paper with watercolor paints. When dry, trace around the leaf shapes and draw veins with a fine- or medium-point permanent marker.

Wiggle Leaf Design

- Using the black marker, trace around two or three leaves (and no more) on paper. Color each leaf with crayons or markers.
- With a crayon or colored pencil, trace just beyond the leaf shape by ½" or so, following the shape, but not touching it. Then trace around this line, about ½" or more, expanding out from the original leaf.
- Do the same around each leaf with ever-expanding lines. As the expanding lines grow, lines will at some point bump into each other. Make an artistic decision about when to stop drawing lines. Even if they cross over each other, the design will be interesting and look "wiggly," like an optical illusion.

Melted Leaf Mobile

Note: Although the warming tray will not get very hot on the "warm" setting, it is important to have an adult nearby at all times and to wear protective mittens or work gloves for this activity.

- Place a large leaf on an electric buffet warming tray (ask an adult to set the temperature on "warm"). Leaf shapes cut from paper are equally effective for this activity.
- Use a crayon to draw on the leaf. Allow the warm tray to melt the crayon as you slowly color the leaf or paper leaf shape. Try mixing several colors on the leaf if desired.
- Remove the leaf and set it aside. Color several more leaves in the same way.
- Attach each leaf to a tree branch with a different length of string, thread, or yarn so the leaves hang down at various levels. To hang this tree branch mobile, tie string to each end of the branch (or paper towel tube) and join them above.

Note: Electric buffet warming trays are usually available in thrift stores and yard sales. Warming trays are easy to clean: While the surface is still warm, wipe off the warm crayon with an old towel or paper towels. If you use the tray only for art, detailed cleaning is not necessary. If you plan to use the tray for non-art related activities, cover it with foil before using it for this activity.

Lids (from frozen juice cans)

Use juice lids for metallic art experiences, including lid stencils and lid magnets.

Materials for Day 1 | lids from frozen juice cans • crayons, markers, permanent markers tempera paint, watercolor paint, acrylic or BioColor® paint, and paintbrushes • white glue, masking tape • drawing paper, colored paper, newsprint or butcher paper • scissors

Materials for Day 2 | lids from frozen juice cans • masking tape • butcher paper or other large paper • tempera paint or watercolor paint, and paintbrushes

Materials for Day 3 | masking tape • large sheets of paper • tempera paints and paintbrushes • optional—squares of white copier or printer paper, water in a cup and a brush, or small spray bottle

Materials for Day 4 | collage materials— choose from: shells, glitter, fabric shapes, confetti, sequins • string, ribbon, yarn • scissors • white glue • magnetic craft strips (small magnets require adult use of glue gun) • optional—hammer and nail, pushpins; string, ribbons, or yarn

Materials for Day 5 | lids from frozen juice cans (plain or previously decorated) • suitable work surface • flat piece of wood or flat board • short nails with wide heads— consider using roofing nails • hammer • optional—collage materials (see suggestions for Day 4)

DAY 1

Lid Art Explorations

- Try any of the following art ideas, or combine two or more of the ideas in one activity!
  - *Permanent Markers:* Draw on a lid with permanent markers.
  - *Acrylic Paint:* Paint on a frozen juice lid with BioColor® paint or acrylic paint, which will look shiny and cover well.
  - *Circle Template:* Trace a lid to make circles all over a piece of paper, and then decorate the circles with crayons, markers, or paint.
  - *Circle Design:* Glue or tape lids to paper to make a design, or draw on a small circle of paper and glue it to a lid.
  - *Trace, Draw, and Stick:* A simple, fun combination of techniques is to trace lids on colored paper to make circles. Then draw on lids with markers and glue the lids (or use loops of tape) into the circles.

DAY 2

Stencil Lids

- Tape lids to a sheet of butcher paper or other large paper using loops of masking tape on the back of the lid. Tape them in a design or pattern, or tape them randomly.
- Paint over the lids and onto the paper between them. Paint with as many colors as desired. Then let the painting dry.
- Remove the lids, and white circles will be left where the lids once were.
- Wash and dry lids, and use for Lid Prints on Day 3.

Lid Prints

- With loops of masking tape, stick several lids to a large sheet of paper spread on a table. Use as many as will fit on a sheet of paper. Paint the lids with tempera paints.
- Press another large sheet of paper over the lids and pat and rub the paper with your hands. Peel away the paper and lift a print. You can make smaller prints by pressing squares of white copier or printer paper over individual painted lids. If the paint dries out, refresh the painted lid with a little water on a brush or from a small spray bottle. Then make more prints!
- It is inspiring to experiment with mixing colors on the lids and then to notice what happens to the prints.

Lid Magnet Craft

- Decorate a frozen juice can lid using glue and collage materials, forming any design. Use whatever small collage materials might be on hand, like shells, glitter, fabric shapes, confetti, sequins, or other suitable materials. Let the collage dry well.
- Place a small magnetic strip on the back of the lid. The lid will stick to a refrigerator door or other appropriate metal surface for display. If the lid is too heavy, add additional magnetic strips until strong enough.
- *Hanging Lid Idea:* Ask an adult to hammer a hole in a lid near the edge. Tie string or yarn through the lid and hang it from a pushpin.
- *Lid Garland Idea:* Before decorating the lids, ask an adult to hammer holes in a few lids. String several lids in a series on a long line of yarn, ribbon, or heavy string. Be sure to tie knots between the lids so they don't slide back and forth. Drape the garland around a window or any other place where it can be viewed and appreciated.

Pounded Lid Relief

Safety note: This activity requires help and supervision by an adult at all times.
- Work on a surface that is suitable for hammering and nailing. Work with plain or previously decorated lids. Begin by arranging the lids on a flat piece of wood (12" x 12" is a good size, but any size will work fine, even a long board). Consider painting the wood or covering it with an original painting, or use the wood as is.
- Ask an adult to provide guidance and supervision as you hammer one nail through a lid and into the wood. Hammer the nail all the way in if you want the lid secured to the wood, or nail the lid partway into the wood to leave the lid loose and jangly.
Hint: Nails should be no longer than the depth of the wood so they will not go through the wood and out the other side.
- Fill the board in any design. Add other collage items or paint.

Magazines

Magazines and catalogs are packed with colorful pictures that are great for collages and other art explorations.

Materials for Day 1 | magazine or catalog pictures featuring one main color • scissors • white paper, drawing paper, or cardboard • glue or glue stick • white glue thinned with water, and a brush

Materials for Day 2 | selected pictures from magazines and catalogs • scissors • choose from paste, white glue, or glue stick • drawing paper or other paper • drawing tools—choose from: markers, colored pencils, crayons

Materials for Day 3 | all the pages from a magazine • pencil, soda straw, chopstick, or thin dowel • clear tape • for the base—choose from: cardboard, box lid, paper plate

Materials for Day 4 | magazine pages rolled into tubes (see Day 3) • pencil, soda straw, chopstick, or thin dowel • white glue • soup can or other can • scissors • optional—glue gun (adult use only) • hobby coating (such as Mod Podge®), and brush

Materials for Day 5 | magazine or catalog pictures that look like fun • background: any paper, cardboard, back of a used poster • scissors • paste, white glue, or glue stick

DAY 1

Color Collage

- Decide on one color for the Color Collage. Tear or cut pictures from magazines that feature that one color; include objects, people, landscapes, and so on.
- Cut around the pictures, keeping some large and others small. It is best to start with larger pieces to cover a good portion of the background, and then add smaller ones on top of this, overlapping the pieces and using other pieces to fill in spaces.
- Glue the magazine pictures on white paper or a piece of cardboard. To seal the pictures in and give them a shine, brush a layer of white glue thinned with water over the entire collage. Let dry overnight.

Note: Collage comes from the French word "coller," which means "to glue."

DAY 2

Clipping Drawing

- Clip a picture of an animal head (such as a cat, dog, or other animal) from a magazine. Glue the clipping to a sheet of paper. Look at the clipping and imagine the rest of the picture that is missing.
- Draw the details to complete the picture, incorporating that animal's head in some way by adding details and interesting ideas. Some ideas are: draw a fancy ball gown and tiara for the cat, draw an ocean wave and show the dog surfing, draw a mouse reading a book, a cow dancing in a ballet tutu, and so on.
- Use crayons, markers, or colored pencils, to add as many details as you like. Most artists like to make their drawings humorous.

Magazine Tube Sculpture

- Tear all of the pages from a magazine and stack them in a pile. Make magazine "tubes." Place a pencil (soda straw, chopstick, thin dowel) diagonally across a corner of one magazine page. Roll the paper around the pencil all the way across the page, creating a tube. Hold the rolled tube lightly so the pencil can fall out.
- Tape the loose end corner of the roll in the center of the tube. Make at least 10 tubes, but many, many tubes are even better. Everyone can help roll magazine page tubes!
- To build a sculpture, simply join the tubes together with tape. Build something on a paper plate or cardboard square, or work without a base. Anything goes. Tubes can bend, and one tube can slip inside another to make an extra long tube. Most artists like to build abstract sculptures; others create a more realistic creation like a horse or a rocket ship. Add collage materials or yarn to complete the sculpture.

Rolled Container Craft

- With your tube rolling experience from Day 3, making a container covered in rolled magazine tubes will be easy and fun! Tear colorful pages from magazines as usual. Begin rolling the page around a pencil as before, but this time, once the paper wraps completely around the pencil one time, spread glue over the remainder of the magazine page. This will make the tube extra strong. Pull out the pencil.
- Make rolled magazine tubes until there are enough to go around a soup can in a "soldier row" (tubes standing up straight).
  Note: Although the magazine tubes will stick to the can if you take the label off, the tubes stick best if you leave the label on the can.
- Glue the rolled magazine pages on the can, or ask an adult to use a glue gun to stick the rolled pages to the sides of the container.
- Tubes may stick up beyond the top and bottom of the can, so snip off the ends of the rolls, making the rolls even with the can's top and bottom edges.
- Paint over all the rolls with a clear hobby coating like Mod Podge® and dry overnight. Use the container for pencils, art supplies, or other uses.

Silly Magazine Mix-Up

- The idea of a Magazine Mix-Up picture is to make a humorous artwork combining different pictures from magazines, such as making a body from a candy bar with the head of a tiger and ears made of bicycle tires, and so on. Choose from a pile of magazine pictures that look like fun.
- Cut one part from one magazine picture, like a tiger's head. Cut more pieces from other pictures, like a baby's shoe or a bottle of juice. Glue the first piece to the background paper.
- Choose another unrelated magazine picture, and glue that part to the first, building the silly picture. Imagine a bowl of ravioli for the face of a girl, with a palm tree for her body, standing on a mountain range for her floor. Part of the fun is imagining the picture you will create while looking through magazines finding and tearing out pages and pictures.

Magazines

Masking Tape

Let your artistic freedom be inspired by the many ways masking tape can be used.

Materials for Day 1 | masking tape (regular beige variety) • scissors • drawing paper • coloring choices: markers, crayons, chalk, food coloring, liquid watercolor paint • color rubbing choices: tissue, cotton ball, cosmetic pad or sponge • optional—copier or printer paper, peeled crayons

Materials for Day 2 | masking tape (regular or colored) • cardboard paper towel tube base (see Day 2 for ideas) • scissors • collage materials (see Day 2 for ideas) • art tissue • optional—sequins, glitter, white glue

Materials for Day 3 | masking tape (any variety) • large sheet of paper or colored • poster board • crayons • optional—tempera paints or liquid watercolor paints, and paintbrushes

Materials for Day 4 | masking tape (standard beige or any color) • tall can (from soup, beans, coffee) • scissors • collage materials (see Day 4 for ideas) • white glue or tape • filler for can, choose from: handmade paper, flowers, pipe cleaners, and photographs

Materials for Day 5 | masking tape (standard beige or any color) • drawing paper or other strong paper • scissors • optional—coloring materials, choose from: chalk, crayons, markers, watercolor paint and brush

DAY 1

Tape & Color

- Tape pieces of standard beige masking tape to a sheet of heavy paper or construction paper, crossing the pieces over one another in any design. Leave spaces between the pieces of tape where parts of the paper are not covered.
- Use markers or crayons to color the spaces between the pieces of masking tape. To color the masking tape, rub it with colored chalk, or with a cotton ball dipped in food coloring or liquid watercolor paint. (Blend the chalk with a tissue or cotton ball.) Use one or all of these methods on the same design.
- *Crayon Rubbing Idea:* Place plain paper over the masking tape art and make a crayon rubbing of it. To do this, rub the plain paper with a peeled crayon held on its side. The tape design underneath will appear as you rub the crayon back and forth over the paper.

DAY 2

Masking Tube Sculpture

- Cover paper towel tubes with beige or colored masking tape. First, tape the tube in a standing position onto a square of matboard, a paper plate, or other sturdy paper. Then begin wrapping the tube from the bottom up with a long piece of tape. As you wrap the tape around the tube, tuck in curled scraps of paper (or fringed or folded paper) so the scraps stand out from a seam of the tape. Tuck in feathers or other collage materials like craft sticks, ribbons, aluminum foil, artificial flowers, buttons, cotton balls, glitter, lace, sequins, yarn, or pipe cleaners as you wind the tape around the tube.
- Continue wrapping and tucking in materials from the bottom up, filling it with bright and unusual attachments. When you reach the top of the tube, the sculpture is nearly complete.
- To finish, stick some art tissue in the hole at the top of the tube so it stands out of the hole. Facial tissue or aluminum foil would also work well. Fluff it out at the top, and the sculpture is complete.
- *Add Shine Idea:* A little glitter or some sequins can be added with dots of glue.

Multi-Scribble over Tape

- Make a design on a big piece of paper with different lengths of masking tape.
  Hint: Pat the tape down lightly because you will need to remove it in a few minutes. Place the tape pieces over each other, side by side, or in any design. Be sure to leave paper showing between tape pieces!
- Grab a handful of crayons, enough to make a true handful. Using all the crayons in your hand, scribble over the entire tape design, around and around, over and over, in and out, here and there, filling the paper with multicolored scribbles.
- Carefully and gently remove all the tape. Stenciled white areas will be left where the tape used to be.
- *Bonus Idea:* Repeat this activity using paints rather than crayons.

Sticky Can Collage

- Select a clean, dry, tall can, such as a soup, fruit, or coffee can. To make a collage using the can as a base, completely wrap tape around the can, with the tape's sticky side out. Wrap the tape around and around until the entire can is covered, even the top edge.
- Create a design on the sticky can by attaching materials to the tape, such as feathers, buttons, sequins, photos, glitter, lace, ribbons, sewing trims, stickers, magazine clippings, cotton, yarn, and so on. Cover the entire can. Use glue or more tape to add additional materials.
- Put something in the can or leave it empty. Some ideas for fillers include handmade paper flowers or pipe cleaners with small photos glued on the ends. You can also use the can as storage for pencils or markers.

Masking Tape Drawing

- To make a "tape drawing," think of pieces of masking tape and how they will become the lines of a drawing. In other words, you will "draw with tape." Press long pieces of tape on a big sheet of paper or a sheet of poster board. Twist and curve the tape, bending and stretching it to form a picture with tape lines. Work the tape to make curves or any other kinds of lines. Press the tape firmly so it adheres well to the paper. Cut the tape into narrow pieces or different lengths as needed.
- When the tape drawing is complete, trim any ragged tape ends.
  Note: Some artists like to add color to the paper with chalk, crayons, markers or watercolor paint.

Masking Tape

69

Newspaper

Enjoy an entire week of papier-mâché! First make homemade papier-mâché paste and then work with newspaper strips to form a papier-mâché box. Make sure to have an area where you can create with papier-mâché and another one where your creations can dry for a few days.

Materials for Day 1 | flour, water • bowls, measuring cups, wooden spoon • saucepan and stove (for adult use only) • powdered cinnamon or peppermint extract • covered bowl • refrigerator

Materials for Day 2 | torn newspaper strips • tissue box for the papier-mâché form, or another box or a balloon • papier-mâché paste, from Day 1

Materials for Day 3 | continue adding torn newspaper strips with papier-mâché paste, from Day 1 • additional newspaper for newspaper pulp • large bowl • hot water

Materials for Day 4 | newspaper pulp, continued from Day 3 • white glue • waxed paper

Materials for Day 5 | acrylic paints and brushes • spray gloss hobby sealer, or hobby coating and a brush (Mod Podge®)

DAY 1

Part 1
Cooked Papier-Mâché Paste

- Measure 1 cup flour and 5 cups warm water, but do not mix them yet. Pour four cups of water in a saucepan (set aside the fifth cup).
- In a medium bowl, mix the remaining one cup of warm water into the one cup of flour, stirring vigorously to remove lumps.
- **Adult Step:** Ask an adult to boil the four cups of water in a pot on the stove, and then slowly add the flour-water mixture to the boiling water, stirring. Mix well and boil for another 2–3 minutes stirring continuously. The paste should be smooth and thick. Add cinnamon or peppermint extract to keep the fragrance of the wet glue fresh. Allow to cool.
- The cooked paste is ready to make papier-mâché! When not in use, store it in a refrigerator in a covered bowl. (This recipe can be doubled or halved if needed.)

DAY 2

Part 2
Make a Papier-Mâché Box
(A WEEK-LONG PROJECT)

- Follow these easy steps to create a papier-mâché box from a tissue box. You may choose another kind of box—like a cereal box, a shoebox, or a milk carton. A balloon will also work. Because this project will take most of the week to complete, set aside an area that can handle an ongoing papier-mâché project for the entire week.
- Tear (do not cut) newspaper into strips. Dip one strip of newspaper at a time into the paste that was cooked on Day 1. Pull the saturated strip through two fingers to squeeze off excess paste in the bowl. Stick the newspaper strip over the tissue box (or other form) and smooth it down with your fingers. The paste washes off hands easily.
  Hint: Newspaper tears easily in one direction, but not in the other.
- Continue with this process until you completely cover the box with one layer of overlapping newspaper strips. Dry for 24 hours.
- On Day 3, add another layer of newspaper strips and let dry another 24 hours. On Day 4, repeat this process. There should be at least three layers. On Day 5, paint the finished box and decorate it.

Papier-Mâché Layer 2 and Newspaper Pulp Sculpture Preparation

- Add another layer of papier-mâché to the tissue box (or other box) and set it aside. Begin the pulp sculpture activity.
- **Preparation of Pulp for Newspaper Pulp Sculpture for Day 4:** Tear about eight sheets of newspaper into 1" strips. Cut those strips into little ½" bits and place in a large bowl. Cover the bits with hot water and let soak overnight. The paper will start to look like pulp, which will be used on Day 4.

Papier-Mâché Layer 3 and Part 2 of Newspaper Pulp Sculpture

- After adding the third layer of papier-mâché to the tissue box, set it aside and continue with the newspaper pulp sculpture project.
- *Newspaper Pulp Sculpture:* Work the pulp through your fingers, breaking down any large lumps so that the mixture looks like gray mush. (An adult can use an electric mixer.)
- When the lumps are gone, take a big handful of pulp and squeeze and squeeze out all the extra water. Work the pulp by hand. After you have squeezed out all the water, add white glue to this mixture (think 1 part glue to 4 parts pulp).
- Form a ball of the pulp mixed with glue and then place the ball on waxed paper. Press, flatten, and sculpt the pulp into the shape of the object you want to create. Keep the object to about 1" thick (1" objects have a quicker drying time than thicker objects). Let dry for several hours.
- When the pulp is dry, paint the object with acrylic paint. To finish the sculpture, ask an adult to spray it with gloss sealer or hobby coating. Make as many pulp sculptures as the recipe will allow, depending on how big the handfuls are. **Note:** You can also mold and model the pulp into one large sculpture that will take several days to dry.

Papier-Mâché Box Completion

- Paint the papier-mâché covered box with acrylic paints. Acrylics are best because they are shiny, help seal the newspaper, and will not rub off when the box is dry.
- After the paint is dry, a layer of Mod Podge® or other hobby coating (ask an adult to do this step) will protect the surface for years to come.

Newspaper

Paper Plates

Plain paper plates are not plain when they are used for art! Common thin-style or extra heavy, round or square, patterned or plain—all paper plates are art treasures.

Materials for Day 1 | 2 heavy paper plates • glue • scissors • yarn in many colors • optional collage materials—choose from: foil, cotton balls, paper scraps, feathers

Materials for Day 2 | thin paper plates • (adult help required) electric frying pan, heavy aluminum foil, and oven mitts • tape • crayon stubs, peeled • optional—scissors

Materials for Day 3 | thin paper plates (decorated plates from Day 2 may be used) • watercolor paints and paintbrushes • scissors • paper clip and thread for hanging

Materials for Day 4 | 2 paper plates • fish shape cut from colored paper • scissors • white glue, thinned with water, and a brush collage materials—choose from: sand, glitter, foil, cotton balls, paper scraps, sequins, buttons • art tissue or crepe paper • plastic wrap or cellophane • tape, if needed • stapler

Materials for Day 5 | paper plates • pencil • scissors • watercolor paints and paintbrushes • paper towels • decorating materials (see Day 5 for ideas) • stapler, tape, glue • painter's stir-stick

DAY 1

Wrap-Weave Paper Plates

- To prepare, nest two heavy paper plates together, one inside the other and then glue them together to make a double-strong unit. Snip slits around the outside edges of the double plate, about ½" deep and 1" or so apart. An adult may need to help with this step.
- Use a wide array of colored yarn for weaving. To begin, slip the end of a strand of yarn into a slit in the plate, and then pull the strand to another slit somewhere on the plate and tuck it in. Yarn strands will cross over one another, building a weaving of color and texture. Continue wrapping the yarn through the slits, changing colors whenever desired, and tucking yarn into the slits again and again. Many artists like to go over the back as well as the front of the plate as they wrap-weave. Leave the loose ends as they are or tape them to the back of the plate.
- *Collage Embellishment Idea:* Tuck paper scraps, cotton balls, or other materials into the wrap-weaving to add interest. Some artists like to fill the plate until it is thick and puffy with yarn; others like to leave white spaces showing, sometimes coloring those spaces with markers.

DAY 2

Fried Paper Plate with Crayon

Note: For your safety, ask an adult to provide guidance and supervision as you do this activity. Although the electric frying pan is only warm, it is safest to work one on one and to protect your hands with work gloves or oven mitts.

- **Adult Step:** Cover the inside of an electric frying pan with heavy aluminum foil. Tape the cord to the table for safety and cover the heat control (set on "warm") with tape so it cannot be turned to a higher temperature.
- Place a thin paper plate in the pan and let it warm. Wear hot mitts or work gloves for protection as you color slowly on the warm plate with peeled crayon stubs. The crayon will melt as you move it, soaking color into the plate. The design will become transparent.
- When satisfied with the design, remove the plate. Hold it up to the light to see the colors glow. Display the plate in a window, or consider cutting it into a spiral. (See Day 3, Paper Spiral Plate.)

DAY 3

Spiral Plate

- Paint a thin paper plate in any way with watercolors (or use the plate from Day 2). It is not necessary to paint a picture, just let the paint colors mix and swirl.
- When the plate is dry, cut it into a spiral starting at the outside edge, cutting inward towards the center.
- Hang the spiral from an unbent paper clip or thread. Some spirals will be long, some will be short, and all will be colorful.

DAY 4

Fishy Plate Craft

- Cut out a paper fish and glue it to a paper plate. When the Fishy Plate Craft is complete, this fish cutout will resemble a fish in an aquarium.
- Paint white glue thinned with water on the plate, and add torn tissue or crepe paper to suggest seaweed. Glue some sand to suggest the aquarium bottom. Add other collage materials or more fish. Sequins or small buttons suggest bubbles; glitter adds shine to the fish's scales. Add more glue as needed. Set aside briefly.
- Cut the center out of a second paper plate, leaving a narrow border. Glue or tape clear plastic wrap or cellophane over the hole (on the eating side). Turn the plate over and sandwich it to the first plate.
- Staple both plates together all around. Look through the clear plastic, and see how the fish scene sandwiched within the plates looks like it is in an aquarium.

DAY 5

Mask on a Stick

- **Adult Step:** Mark and cut out two eyeholes in a paper plate so the artist is able to see through the holes.
- Turn the plate over so the "food side" is face down on your workspace. Paint the paper plate with watercolors to give it a color base. Dab away extra moisture with paper towels if needed. (Paint should dry quickly.)
- Decorate the plate in any way. Some artists like to create an animal or character; others like to explore a more abstract use of materials. Some ideas include gluing or stapling crumpled art tissue for hair, drawing features with permanent markers, adding facial features with paper scraps, or adding yarn, glitter, foil, cotton balls, or other collage materials that are interesting to you.
- When complete, ask an adult to staple or tape a painter's stir-stick to the undecorated side of the plate. You can hold up the plate-mask and look through the eyeholes in the style of a masquerade party mask.

Photographs

Photographs tend to pile up, especially if they are duplicates or blurry shots. Digital photographs printed in black and white or color are useful and fun art materials.

Materials for Day 1 | box of photographs that are old, unused, extras, duplicates, blurry, or of unknown people, pets, or scenes • shoebox • jar lid • pencil or pen • scissors • white glue, glue stick, tape • crayons, markers • optional—clear contact paper • optional—other boxes, like a tissue box or cereal box

Materials for Day 2 | photographs of family and pets • poster board • scissors • glue or tape • optional—cardboard box

Materials for Day 3 | discarded photographs • scissors • glue • drawing paper • optional—magazine or catalog pictures

Materials for Day 4 | digital photos printed from the computer on regular paper (not photo paper) • scissors • thinned white glue and brush • glue stick • several sheets of newspaper, or newsprint

Materials for Day 5 | photographs that are old, unused, extras, duplicates, or of interesting scenes • pictures from magazines or catalogs • scissors • crayons, markers • white glue or glue stick • drawing paper • a photo of yourself

DAY 1

Photo Collage Box

- Because photos can be so much fun and inspiring for art, creating a place to keep them is important. Find a sturdy shoebox and cover it with photographs that have been cut in any way. (Photos cut in circles are cheerful and attractive. Select a jar lid or other circle templates to place on a photo and trace that shape around the important subject of the photograph, then cut along the line to ensure an exact shape.)
- Glue the photos to the box, overlapping the edges so the box is well-covered. Cover the lid too. Let the box dry overnight.
- The next day, fill the box with extra photos that can be used for art. Begin with the project on Day 2 called Family Finger Puppets!
- *Preserving Idea:* Cover the box with clear contact paper to help preserve the photos and keep the box sturdy and smooth.
- *Other Boxes Idea:* Because using photos to make a collage on a box is so easy and so much fun, think about covering a tissue box or even a cereal box too!

DAY 2

Family Finger Puppets

- Cut several lengths of poster board about 1"–2" wide and 4"–6" long, or to lengths that will fit comfortably around your finger. Glue or tape them in circles so they resemble wide rings.
- Cut out photos of family members, pets, or friends. Glue or tape the photos to the loops of poster board.
- Slip the rings on and make up stories and plays with the finger puppets. Some artists may want to make a simple "stage" to perform the plays, using a cardboard box for a theatre. Other artists may want to play music or make up dialogue. From simple to grandiose, imagining with finger puppets is fun to do.

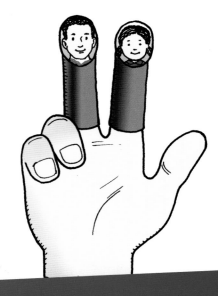

Head & Shoulders, Knees & Toes Art

- Assemble several photos that you no longer need: extra photos, used or damaged photos, blurry photos, or doubles. Cut the people, pets, friends, and family members out of the photos. Then cut them apart, snipping off a head or torso, a tail or four legs, and so on.
- Glue the photos back together on drawing paper, mixing parts in funny ways, like a dad's head on a mom's body, an animal tail on a good friend, or your own head on an elephant. Adding magazine pictures will increase the possibilities. The mixing and creating will bring laughs and fun to all. This activity is perfect for April Fool's Day!

Photo Gift Wrap

- Ask an adult to help you print digital photos from the computer. The photos can be in color or black and white.
  Note: Print the photos on regular paper instead of thicker photo paper so they will bend and fold easily.
- Use a brush and white glue thinned with water to glue a selection of photos to a large sheet of newspaper or newsprint, completely covering the paper. Make several sheets if possible. Let the paper dry overnight before using it as wrapping paper.
  Hint: Make small gift wrap by printing out photos and using a glue stick to glue them to a smaller piece of paper. In fact, one photo can wrap a small gift without any collage work.

My Photo & My Trip

- Select a piece of paper. Draw or create a collage of a real or imaginary place to visit. To do this, cut out scenery, or parts of scenery, from photographs or from magazines. Draw other details or whatever the scene needs to make it complete.
- To finish the artwork, cut out a picture of yourself and glue it into the scene. For example, put yourself on a snowy mountaintop in the Rockies, on the rings of Saturn, or design a world with pictures of yummy desserts as your furniture and pictures of soda bottles as your lamps.

Photographs

Plastic Bottles

Clear plastic bottles come in all sizes, from small, individual water bottles to larger soda and beverage containers. Individually sized bottles are especially nice for art activities.

Materials for Day 1 | plastic drinking bottle with screw-on cap • shiny collage materials (see Day 1 for ideas) • white glue • scissors

Materials for Day 2 | plastic drinking bottle with screw-on cap • shiny, waterproof collage materials (see Day 2 for ideas) • water and glycerin • optional—food coloring • masking tape or duct tape

Materials for Day 3 | plastic drinking bottles, plastic bottles of any kind • liquid watercolors, tempera paints, and paintbrushes • shallow trays for paint • stick-on materials (see Day 3 for ideas) • dowel and duct tape

Materials for Day 4 | large plastic bottle with screw-on cap • box of toothpicks • craft rice • duct tape or masking tape • colored paper or drawing paper • stickers or other decorations • marker

Materials for Day 5 | plastic drinking bottles, plastic bottles of any kind, with lids • nail or push pin (adult step) • colored sand (purchased or homemade, see Note) • small metal or plastic funnel • smooth place on the ground outdoors • tape • optional—white glue and paintbrush, cardboard

DAY 1

Stuffed Bottle

- Use shiny scraps, confetti, glitter, foil paper, candy wrappers, sequins, ribbons, crinkled paper, and other scraps to fill a clear, dry plastic water bottle.
- Screw the lid onto the bottle. Color the lid with markers, or leave it plain. Add more ribbons and materials on the outside of the bottle if desired.
- Line up several similarly filled and designed bottles in a window and enjoy seeing the variations in color and design.
  Note: Plan ahead before beginning the activity: make sure the bottles are completely clean and dry, including the lids.

DAY 2

Bottle with a Shiny View

- Fill an individual-size plastic water bottle loosely with glitter, gold foil paper, gold coin wrappers, sequins, bits of drinking straws, cellophane, ribbon, shredded (pink, white, purple, blue) plastic bags, and snips of clear plastic wrap.
- Fill the bottle almost ¾ full with water, add a little glycerin, and, maybe a drop of food coloring. Use the smallest drop of food coloring possible or the color may obscure the view.
- Put the top on tight and seal it with masking tape or duct tape. Repeat the process with several bottles, and enjoy turning them and looking at the colors and shiny things moving inside the bottles.

Note about colored sand: You can purchase colored craft sand at craft stores or school supply stores, or you can make it by mixing sand with crushed colored chalk. Another way is to mix sand with liquid watercolors in a bowl, and then let the sand dry on newspapers or a cookie sheet overnight. It is best to use clean, purchased sand, pre-colored or colored by you. If you use sand from the beach or a river, be sure to sift it to remove debris. To sanitize beach or river sand, ask an adult to bake it for fifteen minutes in the oven in a baking pan, and then let the sand cool before using it.

Bottle Prints

- Try one of the following ideas to make bottle prints, or try your own idea.
  - *Circle Print Idea:* Dip the opening of the bottle in thick paint, and then press the bottle onto paper, making a little circle design. Dip in many colors and fill the paper with circles. Try the bottom of the bottle too!
  - *Rolled Print Idea:* Roll a plastic bottle in paint, holding the two outside ends. Then roll the bottle on paper. This will make line designs from the ridges on the sides of the bottle. Roll in several colors at once to get a rainbow effect.
  - *Stick-On Print Idea:* Stick bunion pads, corn pads, adhesive bandages, and other thick stick-on materials on the sides of the bottle. Also consider gluing on different shapes and pieces of felt, although they will need to dry for several hours before using. When the bottle is covered with thick pads, roll it in paint and then roll it on paper like a rolling pin. Try two or more colors at once for mixing and blending colors.
  - *Printing Experiment Idea:* Insert a dowel in the bottle and roll the bottle while holding the dowel. This works best if the paper large and positioned on the wall. It helps to use duct tape to secure the dowel to the bottle's opening.

Rain Bottle

- Fill a dry, empty plastic bottle with a box of toothpicks. Then add craft rice to the bottle, leaving a space of about 1 ½" at the top.
- Tighten the lid and seal with tape.
- Gently turn the bottle this way and that, and as the rice falls through the toothpicks, it will sound like a rainstorm.
- To decorate the bottle in a rainy design, cut a 3"–6" x 12" strip of drawing paper. You can draw raindrops and umbrellas or any other rainy designs on the paper; include stickers or other decorations. You can also write the word rain in fancy letters and incorporate it into the design. Then tape the paper around the bottle as a rainy label.

Drawing with Colored Sand Bottles

Note: Ask an adult to use a nail or pushpin to punch a small hole in the bottom of a plastic bottle. (It is best to start small.) Then place a piece of tape over the hole.

- Use a funnel to fill this bottle about half full with colored sand. Repeat this with several bottles, each with a different color of sand. Replace the lids on the bottles. Try one of the following ideas:
  - *Non–Permanent Sand Drawing Idea:* Smooth a place on the ground outdoors. Pull the tape from a bottle and let the sand fall in a design while moving the bottle around slightly above the ground. (If the hole for the sand is not big enough, ask an adult to insert a nail and wiggle it to expand the hole.) Add other colors to the sand drawing until the design is complete. To store the bottles, cover the holes with tape.
  - *Permanent Sand Drawing Idea:* Brush glue thickly on cardboard to cover it completely. Repeat the same bottle technique with the sand, letting the sand fall onto the glue. When the entire design is complete, let the glue dry, then turn and tap the cardboard so the excess sand falls onto newspaper. Save this sand for more art fun.

Plastic Snap-On Lids

Snap–on plastic lids are great for tracing circles, displaying round artwork, and much more. Get ready for a week of creativity using plastic circles!

Materials for Day 1 | plastic snap-on lids • paper • crayons or tempera paints and paintbrushes, or both

Materials for Day 2 | plastic snap-on lid • sturdy paper or poster board • crayons • liquid watercolors or regular watercolors, paintbrushes • ruler or piece of cardboard • tissue or paper towel • crayons, markers • scissors • tape • hole punch • yarn or ribbon • optional—magazine pictures, greeting cards, photos, or drawings

Materials for Day 3 | at least 9 plastic snap-on lids • hole punch (paper punch) • permanent markers or pictures to glue • optional—magazines, photos • crayons, markers • scissors • glue, tape

Materials for Day 4 | plastic snap-on lid • craft mosaic pieces (optional: buttons, small stones, beads, or aquarium gravel) • white glue • hole punch (paper punch) • rag or tissue • yarn

Materials for Day 5 | plastic snap-on lids • hole punch (paper punch) • large paper clip • crayons • facial tissue • yarn or string

DAY 1

Circle Tracers

- Trace a plastic lid on paper. Trace circles all over the paper, in any pattern. Explore overlapping circles to create intersecting shapes.
- Fill in the shapes with color and designs using crayon or paint. (It is interesting to change the color or design where the circles overlap.) Some artists like to add color and design to the background—the areas outside the circles. **Note:** Plastic snap-on lids can be found on coffee cans and on containers of cocoa, dog treats, powdered beverages, snacks, and raisins.

DAY 2

Double-Sided Design Lid

- Trace a plastic lid on sturdy paper, making two separate circles.
- To decorate the first circle, use any art technique. One especially effective technique is to draw with crayon and then paint over the crayon color with liquid watercolors or any watercolor paints. For an extra-cool effect, smear the wet watercolor paint with a ruler or a piece of plastic or cardboard about the size of a credit card to remove extra paint (or dab the paint with a tissue or towel).
- Decorate the second circle design with paint, crayon, or markers.
- Cut both circles out. Glue one on each side of the plastic lid (or use loops of tape to secure the circles). Ask an adult to punch a hole through the circles and plastic lid, and tie a piece of yarn or ribbon through the hole.
- Hang the artwork so that both sides are visible as the circles twist and blow in moving air currents.
- *More Circles Idea:* Cut circles from magazine pictures, greeting cards, photos, or original drawings.

Four Ideas for a Lid Gallery

- Try one of the following ideas:
  - ○ *Grouped Lids Idea:* Collect at least nine plastic lids. Ask an adult to punch holes in each lid, one on the top edge, one on the lower edge, and then punch two more holes, one on the right edge, and one on the left edge. Tie the lids in a 3 x 3 hanging grid. Draw directly on the lids with permanent markers, or glue pictures or drawings on the front and back of each lid (see Day 2). Consider adding lids over time to make a huge wall hanging that is 4 × 4, 5 × 5, or an even larger grid.
  - ○ *Magazine Clips Idea:* Cut out faces from a magazine, and place them on each side of the lids.
  - ○ *Theme Art Idea:* Assemble and design lids that reflect a theme, like "Happiness," "Winter," or "Animals."
  - ○ *Photo Display Idea:* Use the lids to display photos of friends, family, pets, sports heroes, and so on.

Mosaic Circle Craft

- Fill a plastic lid with a puddle of white glue. Press craft mosaic pieces into the glue, filling the lid in any design. No mosaic pieces handy? Use colorful alternative items like aquarium gravel, beads, small stones, or buttons.
- Let the lid dry for several days until the glue turns clear. (It may take as long as a week.)
- Gently peel back the plastic lid and carefully pop the hard circle from the lid. Hold it up to the light to see the patterns, or display in a sunny window. **Note:** An adult can drill or punch a hole through the hard glue. Insert a piece of ribbon through the hole to hang the mosaic circle in a window.

BONUS IDEA

Plastic Lid Creature Craft

Materials | plastic snap-on lids • construction paper • markers • collage items: yarn, googly craft eyes, shredded paper, glitter, buttons, and so on

- Use a plastic lid to create an imaginary Creature Craft: Create a creature that has a round center and arms and legs that extend from the circle. Possibilities include an octopus, a ghost, a spider, or another imaginary creature.

Scrimshaw Lid

- Use a plastic lid as a whole circle, or cut a large shape from the plastic lid. Ask an adult to punch a hole in the lid or the cut-out shape so you can hang it later.
- Unfold a paper clip. Use the end of the paper clip to scratch designs or lines in the surface of the lid. Use firm strokes to scratch into the surface.
- Rub a crayon across the scratches, really hard, to fill in the scratches with waxy color. Use as many crayon colors as desired.
- Rub the crayon lines with a tissue to remove extra color. Crayon will remain in the scratches.
- Tie the plastic lid or shape on a loop of yarn, or string many lids together as a garland.
- Cut strips of construction paper about 1" wide, though any width is fine. Tape strips to the edge of the plastic lid so they hang freely. Use as many strips as your creature has legs.
- Bend or curl the "legs" in any way. (Accordion folds are a favorite technique.) To finish the creature, add collage items like yarn for hair and googly craft eyes. Use markers to draw a face or features on the circle center. Punch a hole, insert a length of yarn, and hang to display.

Plastic Wrap

Clear plastic wrap has many surprising art experiences to offer, such as creating a see-through covering, adding an amazing texture in a painting, or providing fun, fluffy stuff for a mobile.

Materials for Day 1 | long piece of clear plastic wrap • tape • permanent markers (Sharpie®), other markers • scissors

Materials for Day 2 | clear plastic wrap • drawing paper • paint: tempera paint, liquid watercolors, or watercolors • paintbrushes or sponge brush

Materials for Day 3 | plastic wrap • margarine lid, or any other large plastic lid • hole punch (paper punch) • scissors • ribbons • yarn • optional—stapler, tape • optional collage materials—choose from: ribbon, yarn, buttons, paper shapes, cotton balls

Materials for Day 4 | clear plastic wrap • shallow box, or a box lid from a candy box or shoebox • tape and glue • colored paper or gift wrapping paper • scissors • drawing tools, like crayons and markers

Materials for Day 5 | clear plastic wrap • white glue in squeeze bottle • heavy paper plate or grocery tray • a box of salt • liquid watercolors and small brushes • tape

DAY 1

Markers on Plastic

- Tape a long piece of clear plastic wrap to a table or workspace so the plastic wrap will not wiggle or move very much.
- Use good permanent markers to draw on the clear plastic wrap. Water-based markers also work well, but permanent markers provide the most color. Let dry for a few minutes.
- Pull the tape from the table, but keep it attached to the plastic. Carry the plastic wrap to a window and press the tape in place so you can see the sunlight shining through the colors.

DAY 2

Plastic Wrapped Paint

- Use a paintbrush or a wide sponge brush to apply paint generously on drawing paper. The sponge brush will make bold areas of color, called "color blocks."
- Press a sheet of clear plastic wrap on the painting while the paint is still wet. When completely dry, peel off the plastic wrap and see the design that is left on the paper.

Fluff-n-Puff Mobile

- Ask an adult to use a hand-held hole punch to make holes all the way around the edge of a large plastic lid.
- Pull a length of ribbon individually through each hole, leaving plenty of extra ribbon hanging down. Tie each ribbon to the lid.
- Pull some clear plastic from the roll of plastic wrap. Scrunch it into a puffy shape and tie it to one of the ribbons in any way. The scrunched plastic wrap will hang down from a ribbon like a fluffy bow. Tie a fluffy piece of plastic wrap to each ribbon.
- Hang the lid flat from a long loop of yarn tied to the lid. The ribbons and plastic will hang down and look very fluffy and interesting.
- *Collage Embellishment Idea:* Staple, tape, or tie other objects like buttons, paper shapes, or cotton balls to the ribbons. The extra weight will encourage the mobile to hang straighter and move in different ways.

3-D Scene Box

- Create a 3-D Scene Box that expresses your favorite theme, sport, event, imaginary world, or even dream. First, line box or lid with colored paper to make the background and sides and bottom of the scene.
- Draw, cut, and glue scenery on the background. For example, a tropical beach scene might have palm trees, waves, and a big sun. To make things stand out from the background, glue or tape a small loop of paper on the back and then stick this to the background. The item will "stand out" from the background, making it look 3-D.
- Draw and color the main person or character. Cut it out, leaving a flap on the bottom to fold back so the character can stand up. Tape or glue the main character standing towards the front of the scene. Add other things to the scene. For example, the tropical scene might have large flowers, a beach basket or fishing satchel, a beach crab, and so on.
- When the scene is complete, stretch clear plastic over the front of the box so the artwork scene looks like it is behind glass. Tape the plastic in place. Stand the box on its side so everyone can look inside.

Salty Watercolor in Plastic

- Spread newspaper on your workspace to catch extra salt.
- Squeeze white glue from a bottle to draw thick lines on a heavy-duty paper plate or grocery tray. Pour salt over all the glue. Gently tap the plate and let the excess salt fall onto the newspaper (save it for another art experience).
- Gently touch the salty glue with a small paintbrush loaded with liquid watercolors (or drip watercolor paint). Touch just the tip of the brush to the salt, and watch the color shoot into the salt and glue. Add more colors so that all the salt has color in it. Add more glue or salt at any time. Fill part of the plate or the whole plate. Allow to dry.
- Because the salt may eventually crack and fall off the plate, cover the entire artwork with clear plastic wrap. Use a long sheet that will wrap all the way around the art. Tape the plastic wrap on the back of the artwork to help seal and hold firmly. Now you can display the art, which has the appearance of looking through clear glass at the sparkly salty colors. Even if the salt falls off, it will be sealed inside.

Plastic Wrap

Playdough

A little flour, salt, water, and a few minutes are all you need to make and enjoy playdough. But don't stop there! Playdough has many more uses for all ages to explore.

Materials for Day 1 | Best Playdough Ever Recipe ingredients: flour, salt, water, food coloring, cream of tartar (optional), oil, saucepan and stove (adult step), wooden spoon, cutting board • tools for playdough— choose from: rolling pin, plastic knife, fork, cookie cutters, scissors • airtight container or sealable plastic bag

Materials for Day 2 | homemade playdough (Best Playdough Ever Recipe on Day 1)— several colors • Plexiglas® or see-through plastic cutting board

Materials for Day 3 | homemade playdough (Best Playdough Ever Recipe on Day 1) • food coloring or liquid watercolors • pencil • poster board

Materials for Day 4 | homemade playdough (Best Playdough Ever Recipe on Day 1) • garlic press or colander • optional—eggshell halves, very well-washed • paper plate

Materials for Day 5 | homemade playdough (Best Playdough Ever Recipe on Day 1) • baking sheet • tools for playdough (see Day 5 for ideas)

DAY 1

Playdough Play

BEST PLAYDOUGH EVER RECIPE

(To double, triple, quadruple this recipe, multiply the measurements and cook in a larger pan.)

Materials | 1 cup flour • ¼ cup salt • 1 cup water food coloring (paste food coloring results in bright colors) • (optional) 1 teaspoon cream of tartar • 1 tablespoon oil

1. Combine the flour, salt, and cream of tartar (for freshness) in a saucepan.
2. Add and stir in the water, oil, and food coloring until smooth.
3. Ask an adult to stir the mixture over medium heat with a wooden spoon until the playdough forms a ball.
4. Place the dough on a cutting board or countertop and let it cool a little.

- Some tools for fun exploration include a rolling pin, plastic knife, fork, cookie cutters, and scissors.
- Use the playdough for hours of exploration. (Working with the still-warm playdough is extra fun.) Store the playdough in a sealable plastic bag or other airtight container.
- ***Birthday Doughcake Idea:*** To this basic playdough exploration, add birthday props, which may include a cake pan, plastic letters, small silk flowers, pipe cleaners, birthday candles, colored pegs, plastic knife, party plates, party napkins, and so on.

DAY 2

See-Through Dough

- Press playdough pieces onto the back of a square of Plexiglas or a transparent plastic cutting board. Using more than one color is extra inspiring!
- Pick up the transparent board and look at the back now and then during the pressing process. Watch the colors mix and join, and notice how the flat surface makes things look swirly and bubbly.
  Note: The Best Playdough Ever Recipe makes playdough that should last several weeks if you store it in an airtight container. Adult help and supervision is needed to make this playdough. Discard playdough when the odor changes or the dough becomes crumbly.

Fill-In Dough Art

- To make different colors of playdough, begin with about a cup of uncolored playdough or a fist-sized ball. Pinch some of the dough off the ball and put this smaller ball in a dish. Drop some paint or food coloring on it, and knead the color in by hand. Use this dough for the "fill-in art."
- Draw with a pencil on white poster board to make a drawing with bold and simple open shapes. Fill in the drawing with pinches of colorful playdough, pressing the dough to the paper to stick. Not only can playdough be pinched and then pressed, but it can also be smeared or dragged to make color. Use leftover dough for more coloring projects on paper. **Note:** Plasticene® or non-drying play clay also works.

Bird Nest Craft

- Push playdough through a colander or a garlic press to create "strings" of playdough. Use these strings to make a big bird nest. Place the nest on a paper plate or place the nest into the "Y" of a found branch.
- Form playdough eggs to place in the nest. Add a playdough bird to the nest too, or fill the nest with eggs only. To use real eggshells, place a well-washed half eggshell in the nest and then add a baby playdough creature or bird to sit in the egg half. Little playdough bugs or creatures can also go into the nest in addition to, or instead of, eggs or birds.
- *Coiled Nest Idea:* Roll several long snakes of playdough and coil them around and around in any way to make a nest.

Textured Tray

- Cover the entire surface of a large baking sheet with playdough to a thickness of about ½"–1". The playdough can be one color, or mix and swirl several together, like rainbow ice cream. Press the dough on the sheet; pat and flatten it evenly with your hands.
- With a tool like a chopstick or Popsicle stick, press or draw lines to divide the playdough sheet into sections or squares.
- Within each section, create a texture design by pressing objects into the playdough. Each section will be different. Experiment with designs based on whatever tools or objects are available. Some tool suggestions include: spoon, large and small fork tines, Lego dots or bumps, cap of pen or marker, tea strainer, coin, Phillips screwdriver point, toy car wheels, doll feet, Popsicle stick tip, chopstick tip, and so on. Experiment with everyday items and explore possible designs. Because the playdough may be drying out, this is a good final project for the week.
- Let the dough dry in the tray. At some later date, you can remove the dried dough from the tray and discard it.

Playdough

Puzzle Pieces

You can recycle old cardboard jigsaw puzzles with missing pieces into art activities. Puzzles with large or small pieces are equally useful.

Materials for Day 1 | old jigsaw puzzle (complete, no pieces missing) • crayons, markers, permanent markers • puzzle storage: original box, clasp envelope, or sealable plastic bag

Materials for Day 2 | jigsaw puzzle pieces (large and small puzzle pieces) • acrylic paint and paintbrushes • small collage items like buttons, sequins, pompoms, yarn bits • white glue • permanent markers

Materials for Day 3 | jigsaw puzzle pieces (smaller pieces work best) • poster board • crayons or markers • white glue, tape

Materials for Day 4 | jigsaw puzzle pieces (large and small puzzle pieces) • cardboard markers • scissors, or X-Acto knife or other cutting tool (adult use only) • white glue • optional—twine • optional—jewelry craft pin-back or earring backs; old picture frame or homemade cardboard frame

Materials for Day 5 | jigsaw puzzle pieces (large puzzle pieces work best) • paper same size as the finished puzzle • scissors • crayons and markers • white glue and brush • X-Acto knife or other cutting tool (adult use only)

DAY 1

Backwards Puzzle Art

- Find an old, cardboard jigsaw puzzle with large puzzle pieces. Turn all the pieces over on a table and put the puzzle together upside down with no picture showing. (If this is too difficult, put the puzzle together right side up on a sheet of poster board, and then flip it over on the table.) The puzzle should be completely joined together.
- Draw with markers on the back of the old puzzle, making a big picture that covers all the pieces. Some artists like to draw a little picture, make designs, or write letters or numbers on each individual piece. Other artists like to make one large picture covering the entire puzzle.
- After you have colored or decorated all the puzzle pieces, the puzzle is ready to reassemble for fun. Take the puzzle apart again. Mix up the pieces on the table and then put it back together once again, this time with the backwards puzzle design showing! To store, keep the puzzle in the original box, a clasp envelope, or in a heavy sealable plastic bag.

DAY 2

Puzzle People

- The shapes of many jigsaw puzzle pieces look a little like people with heads and little round legs and arms. Spread a selection of old puzzle pieces out on newspaper. Large pieces are easy to work with, but smaller ones are fine too.
- Using a small brush and acrylic paints, paint each piece to become a person, character, animal, or creature. Add features with wiggly eyes or other tiny bits of collage materials, like little pompoms or yarn strands, sequins or buttons, and so on. Some artists like to leave parts of the original color of the puzzle piece showing, using it as bright shirts or trousers for their character. You can use permanent markers to add additional features.

Puzzle Poster Picture

- Spread out an old jigsaw puzzle that is missing a few pieces, and sort the remaining pieces into piles by color. Small puzzle pieces work best. Set the pieces aside.
- Draw a large simple picture on white poster board or cardboard. Details are not necessary.
- Glue the puzzle pieces into the picture to fill the drawing with color. For example, fill a tree drawing with green puzzle pieces for the leaves and brown ones for the trunk, or an apple drawing with red pieces. In addition, you can fill the entire background with puzzle pieces too, so the whole poster is filled with color.
- Use the remaining puzzle pieces to glue a puzzle-piece frame around the edge of the artwork. Feel free to create a frame that has several layers of puzzle pieces.

Note: Some artists like to use pieces that actually fit together to make the frame.

Puzzling Initial Plaque

- Draw the big, bold initial of your name on a piece of cardboard, like A for Anthony, B for Beatrice, or S for Smith. Draw it wide and thick in "block letter style."
- Cut the letter out. (Ask an adult for help, if necessary.)
- Use white glue to stick leftover jigsaw-puzzle pieces onto the initial to fill and cover it. Then add a second layer of pieces, placing them this way and that so they fill all the spaces and the cardboard no longer shows. Let the glue dry completely.
- Add a length of twine taped to the back of the plaque for hanging, or simply lean the plaque against the wall on a shelf. Some artists like to cover the back of the letter too.
- *Jewelry Idea:* Glue a puzzle piece to a pin-back or earring backs to make quick-and-easy jewelry.
- *Revitalized Frame Idea:* Glue puzzle pieces to a scratched or dented picture frame to create a new frame.
- *Homemade Frame Idea:* Cover a homemade cardboard frame with puzzle pieces to use as a frame for any art or photo you choose.

Old Is New Puzzle

Note: Work one on one with an adult to do this activity.

- Find an old cardboard puzzle that you have outgrown, the kind with just a few pieces that are very large. Trim a sheet of paper as large as the exact size of the whole puzzle. Draw a picture on the paper, using lots of color. The more color you use, the more interesting the "new" puzzle will be to take apart and put together.
- Put the puzzle together, with protective newspaper under it. Then, apply glue with a brush over the entire puzzle.
- Press the crayon drawing on the puzzle and pat and smooth to adhere to the glue. Let dry well.
- Ask an adult to use a sharp X-Acto knife to cut around all the puzzle pieces so each piece is separate. Allow the pieces to dry completely. Now you have a brand new puzzle to play with, drawn by you!

Rain

Explore the possibilities of what a week of rain can help create when it falls on paint and other everyday color mediums.

Materials for Day 1 | rain • paper plate (heavy duty, uncoated and not shiny, like Chinet® brand) • colored chalk or chalk pastels • facial tissue or cosmetic sponge • optional—powdered tempera paint, and paintbrush or cotton swab, very small containers

Materials for Day 2 | rain • paper plate (heavy duty, uncoated and not shiny, like Chinet® brand) • crayons • tempera paint, food coloring, liquid watercolors, or watercolor paint • paper towels

Materials for Day 3 | rain • water-based markers (**Note:** Most markers are water-based or water soluble, unless they say "permanent" like Sharpie® markers.) • drawing paper • cookie sheet or plastic tray • paper towels • black permanent marker • optional—watercolor paper • optional—old, dry markers

Materials for Day 4 | rain • water-based markers • small squares of heavy paper • cookie sheet • paper towels • yarn • scissors • paper towel tube • optional—umbrella, blue paper

Materials for Day 5 | rain • large sheet of poster board or foam-core board • easel • tempera paints and brushes • old towel or paper towels

DAY 1

Chalk & Rain

- Carry a heavy-duty paper plate outdoors in the rain. (Plates that are uncoated—not shiny—work best.) Allow the plate to soak well, and then bring it back to your workspace.
- Draw freely with any kind of colored chalk or chalk pastels. The rain-soaked plate will cause the chalk to soften a little and will significantly brighten the chalk marks.
- When the drawing is dry, brush chalk lines with a facial tissue or cosmetic sponges to smooth and blend the colors.
- *Powdered Tempera Brush Idea:* Soak an uncoated heavy-duty paper plate, like Chinet, in the rain. Then place it on a workspace indoors. Dip a paintbrush or cotton swab in a very small container of powdered tempera paint (cap from a water bottle, jar lid, film canister) and then dab the powdered paint on the wet paper plate. Use one or many colors, with a brush for each color.

Hint: Keep art rags and a large container of water handy for rinsing brushes.

DAY 2

Crayon Rainy Resist

- Draw with a white crayon (or use many crayon colors) on a heavy-duty uncoated paper plate, like Chinet.
- Sprinkle a few drops of tempera paint, food coloring, liquid watercolors, or watercolor paint on the plate.
- Carry the plate out into a light rain and watch as the rain hits the color and blurs. Let the raindrops spread out over the crayon design. The paint will resist the wax crayon, creating a crayon resist. When satisfied with the results, hurry back indoors and let the plate dry. If needed, blot excess water or paint with an old towel or paper towels. Some artists like to add to the Crayon Rainy Resist with more paint.

Note about rainy art: If it does not rain and you still want to do these projects, make your own rain! Substitute a hand-held mister or spray bottle filled with water, or hook up an outdoor hose with the nozzle on a light spray setting like "mist." Beach or pool toys that squirt add another element of fun outdoors! **Always remember:** Do not go outside during a thunderstorm.

Rainy Marker Maker

- Rain and water-based markers (not permanent markers) combine to create a rain-spattered drawing. To begin, place a sheet of drawing paper on a cookie sheet or a plastic tray. Draw a simple, bold picture, design, or series of shapes on the drawing paper.
  Hint: Detailed drawings will not work as well as simple, bold drawings or designs.
- Take the marker drawing outside when rain is falling. Light rain is the best choice, but heavy rain is exciting too! Hold the tray out, or set it down on a table or on the ground.
- Watch the drawing to see what the rain is doing to the marker lines. When satisfied with the design results, head back indoors and let the drawing dry. If needed, blot excess water with a paper towel or old art towel. The rain works with the marker drawing to spatter, blend, and blur the colors.
- When the drawing is dry, you may want to trace around the shapes and designs with a black permanent marker to highlight and focus on specific areas of the drawing.
- *Watercolor Paper Idea:* Once the technique is clear, try this art experience on real watercolor paper. The results are even better!
- *Marker Experiment Idea:* Place a sheet of paper on a tray. Arrange old, dry markers on the paper, and place the tray on the ground in the rain. Watch what rain can do to dry markers on paper!

Rainy Art Card Mobile

- Use a water-based marker to draw a design on a small square (2"–3") of heavy paper. Use only one color per square. Make an even number of six or more squares.
- Place all of the squares outdoors in the rain on a cookie sheet. Watch what happens. Bring the sheet in when you are satisfied with how the rain has blurred the designs on the squares. Dry the squares briefly, blotting excess moisture if needed.
- Choose two squares. Place a strand of yarn in between the two squares and "sandwich" the two squares and the yarn with glue. Keep the colorful, rain-splotched sides facing out. Tie the loose end of the yarn to a paper towel tube so the squares hang freely. Do this for other pairs of squares to create a mobile.
- Thread one long piece of yarn through the tube and tie both ends above the tube to create a big loop for hanging the mobile. Adjust the yarn so the tube hangs level and balanced.
- *Raindrop Shapes Idea:* Cut pairs of paper raindrop shapes from sheets of blue paper, or from paper of another color. Sandwich these raindrop cutouts in various places along the yarn strands.
- *Umbrella Mobile Idea:* For a truly rainy day mobile, hang the designs from yarn tied to the points of an umbrella!

Run-Run-Rain Painting

- Attach a large sheet of poster board or foam-core board to an easel. Paint with tempera paints (use a medium consistency, not too thick and not too thin), making large, simple shapes and designs rather than details. Let it dry briefly so it is not too drippy.
- Carry the easel outdoors and set it in the rain. Watch the painting run, run, run! Bring the easel inside and let it dry, dabbing away excess moisture with an old towel. No easel? Make a painting as described, and then carry it outside. Two people can hold a painting at a slight angle so the paint will run down the paper. Any other "slanted" setup will work too, like leaning it against a fence or placing it on an outdoor chair.

Rain

Rocks

Rocks come in many shapes and sizes, from gravel to stones to rocks too heavy to carry. Part of the fun of collecting rocks is scrubbing them in soapy water to prepare them for art projects.

Materials for Day 1 | flat, smooth pebbles or small stones in different sizes • cardboard • scissors • heavy duty aluminum foil • white glue • tape

Materials for Day 2 | rocks and pebbles • shoe box lid • paints—choose from: acrylic paints, metallic paints, nail polish, or clear hobby coating, and paintbrushes • permanent markers • white glue • optional—decorate with sewing trim, colored paper, or aluminum foil

Materials for Day 3 | rocks or stones • pipe cleaners • old photographs • bottle cap or circular object for tracing template • glue

Materials for Day 4 | rocks and stones in different sizes • acrylic paints or tempera paints, and paintbrushes • felt or construction paper • scissors • glue

Materials for Day 5 | rock (potato or egg-sized) • roving wool (craft store or knitting shop) • nylon stocking • warm water • liquid soap

DAY 1

Stone Stack Sculpture

- Collect flat, smooth pebbles or small stones in different sizes. Spread them out on your workspace.
- To make a base for the sculpture, cut a piece of cardboard into a square that is slightly wider than the largest stone. Wrap the square of cardboard with four or five layers of heavy-duty aluminum foil so that the square is thick with foil. Press the largest flat stone into the center of the foil, making a dent, and then remove the stone.
- Squeeze white glue into the dent, and then place the stone in the dent. Let the glue dry for a few minutes, making a strong base for the sculpture.
- Squeeze a dab of glue on the first stone, and place another stone on top of it, using a slightly smaller rock. Let the glue dry for a few minutes. Then continue this process, adding smaller and smaller stones to the stack, letting the glue dry a little between stacking. Also use tape to hold the rocks if the glue is drying too slowly. Remove the tape when the glue dries.
- Build the sculpture from large to small. Let the sculpture dry overnight. Remove any tape. Use glitter glue to add color and sparkle, or leave the sculpture in its unadorned form.

DAY 2

Rock Box

- Collect rocks and pebbles, enough to fill a shoebox lid, placing the rocks side by side in one layer. Wash and dry the rocks well. Spread them on your workspace.
- Use acrylic paints, metallic paints, or nail polish (with adult help and guidance) to paint each rock in a different way. Some rocks need only clear paint or hobby coating. Let each rock dry completely.
- When the rocks are dry, decorate or add details to the rocks with permanent markers. Place each rock in the shoebox lid on a large drop of glue. Let the glue dry overnight.
- *Box Embellishment Idea:* Decorate the edge of the box lid using materials like sewing trim, colored paper, or aluminum foil.

Rocky Photo-Face

- Wrap two or three pipe cleaners around a small rock, twisting them tightly around the rock so they hold the rock securely, and then twist the pipe cleaners' ends so they stick up from the rock base.
- Cut out a face from an old photograph. Place a bottle cap or other circular object around the face and trace the circle around it.
- Cut a scrap of paper the same size and shape as the photo-face. Glue the photo and the paper together, sandwiching them around the end of the pipe cleaner.
- Make a photo-face for each pipe cleaner end. Arrange the photo-decorated pipe cleaners by bending them this way or that so the photos are easily visible.

Stone Fruit Craft

- Collect rocks in different sizes. Look at the rocks and imagine which fruit shapes they most resemble. Some rocks may resemble an apple, pear, plum, strawberry, lemon, watermelon, grape, peach, melon, orange, and so on. Choose a rock and paint it to resemble a piece of fruit!
- To add an extra element to your fruit rock, use glue to attach felt or construction-paper leaves. Display your Stone Fruit Crafts in a basket or bowl.

Felted Rock

- Begin with a clean rock (a baked potato-sized or egg-sized rock). Wrap the rock with small amounts of loose "roving wool," using wisps and fluffs in different colors. Bits of well-shredded yarn can be added too. Continue wrapping the rock until it is completely covered and puffy.
- Stretch a nylon stocking over the rock, and tie a knot as close as possible to the wool-covered rock. Dip the rock in very warm water (warm, but still comfortable for your hands).
- Cover your hands in liquid soap, and rub the rock-nylon stocking package. Do not give up! It takes at least 5–10 minutes of rubbing soap on the rock package to "felt" the wool; 15 minutes is even better. The longer you rub the wool, the better it will be. You can remove the stocking after the first few minutes, but keep rubbing with soapy hands, rolling the rock around, using pressure to squeeze the wool around the rock. Use more soap from time to time to keep your hands soapy throughout this process.
- When done, place the rock in the sun to dry. The colors of the wool will mix and shrink and harden to cover the entire rock in beautiful colors.

Rocks

Salt

Every container of salt is just waiting to pour out its crystals and become part of a sparkly art creation! Salt has a compelling visual quality that will inspire creative painting, sculpting, sprinkling, and assembling.

Materials for Day 1 | salt (basic table salt) • liquid watercolor paint or food coloring • sealable plastic bag for each color • salt shakers • white glue in squeeze bottle • cardboard, matboard, or heavy paper • newspaper or dish

Materials for Day 2 | salt (basic table salt, coarse salt, kosher salt, or rock salt) • watercolor paints and water, small paintbrush • optional—cups of tempera paints each mixed with salt

Materials for Day 3 | salt (basic table salt) contact paper • lightweight cardboard • watercolor paints and brushes

Materials for Day 4 | dough recipe • ingredients: salt (basic table salt), flour, hot water, bowl • toothpick • microwave (adult step) • decorating materials: paints, markers, glitter, sequins and glue • yarn • scissors

Materials for Day 5 | salt paint ingredients: salt (basic table salt), flour, water, food coloring or liquid watercolors • funnel • squeeze bottles or sealable plastic bags • scissors • heavy paper

DAY 1

Salty Sprinkle Glue

- To make colored salt, mix ½ cup salt and ¼ teaspoon liquid watercolor paint, or ½ cup salt and 10 drops of food coloring. Place the colored salt in a sealable plastic bag. Make one bag for each color. Seal each bag, pressing out as much air as possible. Knead and shake the bag until all of the salt is completely colored. Pour the salt onto newspaper and dry for about 2 hours. Then put the dry salt in salt shakers. (If you do not have any salt shakers, ask an adult to make shakers by using a hammer and nail to punch holes in the tops of film canisters or clean pill bottles.)
- Draw with glue in any pattern, from scribbling to a planned picture on cardboard, matboard, or heavy paper (paper plates work well). Shake or sprinkle salt over the glue lines or over the entire paper if desired. Gently tap the extra salt onto a sheet of newspaper or into a dish to use later. Let the glue design dry well.
Note: Salt will fall off if the paper is bent or carried about too much, so keep it flat and still.

DAY 2

Salty Watercolor Painting

- Paint with watercolor paints, using a good deal of water. The painting should be very wet.
- Sprinkle salt on the wet painting. When the painting dries, the salt crystals will leave speckled starburst designs. To see the patterns clearly, brush away the dry salt.
- *Textured Paint Idea:* Mix salt into cups of tempera paint to make a thick, rough-textured paint. When the paint dries, intriguing textures will emerge.

BONUS IDEA

Air-Dry Salt Dough

Materials | ingredients for salt dough: flour, salt, cold water, large bowl, measuring cups • optional—cookie cutters • oven at 200°F • food coloring, or acrylic paint and paintbrush • hobby coating and paintbrush

Mix together 2 cups flour and 1 cup salt in a large bowl. Gradually add ½ cup cold water and mix to a dough consistency. Knead the dough on a flat workspace. If necessary, add a few more drops of water during the kneading, but do not make the dough too moist. When the dough is a good consistency for modeling, use

Sticky Salt Paper

- Peel off the backing from a piece of contact paper (clear is good, but white or any kind is fine). Place this sticky side up on a piece of cardboard for support. Cover the entire sticky side with salt. Gently shake off excess salt.
- Use a brush to paint on the "salt paper" with watercolors. Paint gently and lightly, rather than scrubbing or rubbing the brush into the salt. Let your salty paint creation dry overnight.

it as you would any dough. Roll pieces about ¼"–⅛" thick. Cut with cookie cutters, or mold by hand. Allow the finished shapes a day or two to dry, turning them over now and then to help them dry more quickly. The dough may also be baked at 200°F until hard and brown (ask an adult to help with this step). To pre-color the dough, add paint or food coloring to the water before mixing it with the salt and flour. You can also paint the finished shapes with acrylic paint. To seal objects permanently, ask an adult to paint them on all sides with clear varnish or another hobby coating.

Microwave Salt Dough Craft

- Mix 4 cups flour, 1 cup salt, and 1 ½ cups hot water in a bowl to make a pliable dough. Create ornaments or shapes that are fairly flat, no thicker than ½".
- Use a toothpick to make a hole in each dough shape for hanging. Make the hole large enough for thick yarn because the hole will close up a little when the shapes are baked in a microwave.
- Ask an adult to help you microwave several shapes on a microwave-safe plate for 1–4 minutes. (Most microwaves come with such a plate. Do not use a paper plate or any paper product.) Ask an adult to check if the objects are baking. If not, increase the time by increments of 1 minute until the ornaments are fully baked and hard.
  Note: Microwave power levels differ, so proceed slowly at first.
- Let the shapes cool completely before decorating. To decorate, use paints or markers, or glue on interesting items like glitter or sequins.
- Insert yarn for hanging if you made a hole in the shape. The baked shapes should last for several years if stored in a dry place.

Squeezy Salt Paint

- Mix ½ cup salt, ½ cup all-purpose flour, and ½ cup water until it is the consistency of pudding. Add food coloring or liquid watercolors and mix.
- Use a funnel to transfer the paint to a squeeze bottle. If you do not have a squeeze bottle or funnel, transfer the salt paint mixture to sealable plastic bags, one for each color. Snip off one tiny corner of each bag and set it aside until you are ready to squeeze.
- Make designs by squeezing the mixture onto heavy paper, such as a brown paper bag, cardboard, a paper plate, or some other heavy paper. Let the mixture dry overnight. It is best to use the salt paint in one sitting, although you can store the mixture for several days in the refrigerator in containers that are airtight. If you store the salt paint mixture, stir, shake, or mix it before reusing.

Salt

Sand

Sand—from the sandbox, the beach or shore, the yard, the river, the playground, or even from the hardware store—is a versatile material that adds color and texture to art.

Materials for Day 1 | ingredients for playdough: sand, cornstarch, cream of tartar, hot water, measuring cups, large saucepan, stove (adult only), wooden spoon

Materials for Day 2 | sand • spice containers or salt shakers or improvised shakers (see instructions) • powdered tempera • white glue in a squeeze bottle • heavy paper (cardboard, strong paper plate, tagboard) • tray or newspaper

Materials for Day 3 | colored sand (see Day 2 instructions) • containers—choose from: shakers, bowls, yogurt containers, or paper cups • colored paper in several colors • white glue in a squeeze bottle

Materials for Day 4 | colored sand, at least 3 cups • pencil or pen • colored paper or poster board • white glue in squeeze bottle • tray or newspaper • optional—misting bottle or hand-sprayer, plastic wrap, tape, sealable plastic bag

Materials for Day 5 | colored sand • tape • cardboard • contact paper • optional—sealable plastic bag, scissors

DAY 1

Sand Playdough

- Mix 4 cups sand, 2 cups cornstarch, and 1 tablespoon cream of tartar (optional) in a large saucepan. With adult help, stir in 3 cups hot water. Ask an adult to cook this mixture over medium heat, stirring constantly until the mixture is too stiff to stir. Handle when cool enough (slightly warm but feels great).
Note: Cream of tartar is usually available in the spice section of the grocery store. Leave it out of the mixture if you have trouble locating it.
- Play with and sculpt the Sand Playdough with your hands. Sand Playdough creations will air-dry in a few days.

A note about sand: White, clean sand is available at home supply stores in large bags. Pre-colored sand is available from art and school supply stores and catalogs. To clean and sanitize sand from outdoors, sift the sand through a wire mesh sieve or through your fingers, removing any debris or pebbles. Place the sand in a baking pan and ask an adult to bake it in an oven for 15 minutes at 350°F. Let the sand cool before using.

DAY 2

Dandy Sandy Shaker

- Scoop dry sand into spice containers or salt shakers. (No shakers? Ask an adult to use a hammer and nail to poke a few holes through the lid of a plastic jar. Film canisters with one hole punched in each lid also work well, as do picnic squeeze bottles.)
- Add 2 teaspoons powdered tempera per ¼ cup sand, and stir or shake (cover the holes with your hand) to mix. Add more paint for a brighter color; experiment by starting with only a little powdered paint. To control the sand flow from the shaker, cover some of the holes with tape, leaving only a few holes open.
- Draw designs with glue from a squeeze bottle on heavy paper, tagboard, cardboard, or a strong paper plate. Then direct or shake colored sand over the glue.
- Tap the excess sand off the paper onto a tray (save this for the Day 3, 4, and 5 activities). Proceed with one color at a time until the artwork is complete.
Hint: Pat and dab a scrap of contact paper to clean up any sand on floors or tables. This is a great way to pick up extra sand!

Shapes & Sand Design

- Glue bright, bold cutout paper shapes to a contrasting construction paper background. For example, use yellow on purple, red on blue, or white on black.
- Trace around the edges of the shapes with white glue squeezed from the bottle.
- Shake or pour colored sand onto the glue lines, or use sand in containers from Day 2.
- Tap the excess sand onto a tray (save this to use in the Day 4 or 5 activities). Let the design dry completely, and then display it.

Sand & Glue Drawing

- Prepare more colored sand, or use the sand from the Day 2 activity. Make at least three cups of colored sand.
- With a pencil or pen, draw a simple bold picture on a sheet of colored paper or poster board.
- Squeeze white glue on the lines. Continue by completely filling in one small area of the picture with glue. Use a spoon to pour some colored sand carefully on the glue area. Shake the excess sand back into the cup or onto a tray.
- Fill another part of the picture with glue and then cover it with sand, shaking off the excess once again. Repeat this until the entire picture is covered with glue and colored sand.
  Note: Use the extra mixed sand for today, or save for Day 5.
- Seal the drawings using one of the following ideas:
  ○ *Sprayed Glue:* When the sand drawing is dry, use a hand sprayer to spray it with a mixture of white glue thinned with water. Dry the art once again.
  ○ *Plastic Wrap:* Cover the sand and glue drawing with clear plastic wrap and tape the plastic to the back of the drawing.
  ○ *Sealable Plastic Bag:* Slip the drawing into a large sealable plastic bag, press out the air, and zip the bag closed.

Sticky Sand Art

- Peel the backing off a large piece of contact paper and tape it a piece of cardboard, sticky side up. (Taping the contact paper to a piece of cardboard makes it lie flat as you create your Sticky Sand Art.) Work with colored sand, pouring it or sprinkling it on the contact paper in any design. (Another pouring idea is to put sand in a sealable plastic bag, and cut a small corner from the bag. The sand will flow easily from the hole. Pinch the corner of the bag to stop the flow of sand.)
- Use one of the following ideas:
  ○ *Drawing:* Place a drawing under the contact paper so the design shows through; fill in the shapes with sand. Later, remove the drawing and the sand design will remain.
  ○ *Handprint Stencil:* Place your hand down on the contact paper, and sprinkle sand around it to make a handprint sand stencil. Remove your hand and fill in the handprint with a different color of sand, or leave uncolored. Save the excess sand by pouring it onto a tray and then collecting it in a container.
  ○ *Sealing:* Press a second piece of clear contact paper over the sand design to sandwich the design between the two sheets of contact paper.

Sandpaper

Sandpaper's special appeal is its rough texture, which lends itself especially well to art that uses a rough surface that regular paper just doesn't have. Sandpaper comes in varying levels of texture from fairly smooth to very rough.

Materials for Day 1 | sandpaper, coarse yarn, multiple colors • scissors

Materials for Day 2 | sandpaper • wood scraps, wood blocks • tape • white glue, glue gun (optional, adult use only), tape, or Elmers® Carpenters glue • optional coloring—liquid watercolors, watercolor paints, tempera paints, markers

Materials for Day 3 | sandpaper • old scissors (sandpaper will dull good scissors) • cinnamon sticks • yarn

Materials for Day 4 | sandpaper • old scissors (sandpaper will dull good scissors) • pencil • newsprint • crayon stubs or old crayons, peeled

Materials for Day 5 | sandpaper • crayon stubs or old crayons • newspaper or thin cotton rag • white drawing paper • iron (adult step) • optional—old cookie sheet, old scissors, oven (adult step)

DAY 1

Easy Yarn Art

- Cut multiple colors of yarn into various lengths (no longer than 12" each). Stick a strand of yarn on a large piece of coarse sandpaper, twisting and turning it to make designs. The yarn will stick without glue. Use as much yarn as needed to complete the design.
  Note: This activity can be temporary. You can remove the yarn and use it and the sandpaper for other projects. Some artists like to pull yarn off as well as put it on!

DAY 2

Sand-It Sculpture

- Choose several pieces of wood scraps to make into a wood-scrap sculpture. Glue or tape sandpaper around one block of wood. Use this block to smooth the edges and surfaces of the other wood scraps. Sand all the scraps well. This can take a lot of work and time.
- Glue the scraps together to make a sculpture. Ask an adult to help. A glue gun (adult use only) makes the gluing go faster, but white glue from a squeeze bottle works fine with a little extra drying time. Let dry several hours or overnight.
  Note: You can color the wood scraps before or after gluing, using liquid watercolors, tempera paints, or markers.

Cinnamon Rubbing Mobile

- Use old scissors to cut sandpaper into squares or other shapes. Punch a hole in each shape.
- Draw on the sandpaper shapes with a cinnamon stick, or simply rub a cinnamon stick back and forth to put lots of spicy smell on the sandpaper.
- Cut lengths of yarn in many colors. Tie a piece of yarn through the hole of each shape, and then tie each shape to a stick so the shapes hang down. Fill the stick with additional cinnamon sandpaper shapes attached to colorful yarn, hanging at different lengths in any fashion.
- Tie a long piece of yarn to each end of the stick, joining the ends together above the stick to form a simple hanger. Hang the mobile and enjoy the spicy smell of the cinnamon.

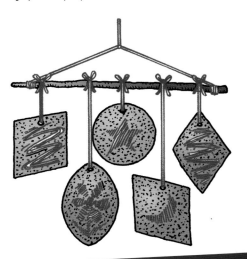

Sandpaper Rubbings

- Use old scissors to cut shapes or letters from a sheet of sandpaper. Use the leftover pieces too. Some artists prefer to draw their shapes first and then cut them out; others like to work freehand.
- Spread the shapes or letters on your workspace. Cover them with a large sheet of newsprint or other paper. Tape the corners of the covering paper to the workspace.
- Peel the paper off a few broken crayons. Turn a crayon on its side and rub over the paper, revealing the bumpy sandpaper beneath the paper. Change colors at any time. The more you rub the design, the clearer it will become. Remove the corner pieces of tape when you are finished.
- Move the shapes or letters around and make a different rubbing. Some artists like to spell their own names, a friend's name, or other words that are interesting or important to them.

Sandpaper Crayon Transfer

- Draw some designs with old or broken crayons on a piece of sandpaper. This in itself is a completed art activity. To transfer the drawing to paper, read further.
- Place the sandpaper design face up on a few sheets of newspaper. Place a piece of white drawing paper over the sandpaper and crayon. Cover this with another piece of newspaper or thin cotton rag.
- **Adult Step:** Set an iron on low (no steam) and press the iron firmly on the stack of papers. Do not wiggle the iron too much; press straight down and move the iron firmly back and forth a little. Peek under the paper to see how the transfer is progressing. Stop ironing after the crayon markings melt and soak into the white paper, transferring the design like a print. Cool briefly before handling.
- *Sandpaper-and-Crayon Bake Idea:* Ask an adult to place the sandpaper drawing on an old cookie sheet in a 225°F oven for a few seconds. Watch for the crayon to melt and spread out on the sandpaper, and then ask an adult to remove the sandpaper art from the oven. Let everything cool before you attempt to handle it. If you are going to cut the sandpaper, remember to use old scissors because sandpaper will dull sharp scissors.

Sandpaper

Socks

Get ready to use socks—stray socks, old socks, outgrown socks, socks without partners—for fine fun art activities!

Materials for Day 1 | socks • sand or lightweight gravel • yarn • optional—needle and thread (adult step) • scissors • large sheet of paper, tape • tempera paint • Styrofoam trays or other shallow tray • optional—outdoor area or cardboard box

Materials for Day 2 | 2 socks • child's plastic darning needle and thread or yarn • scissors • pieces of an old kitchen sponge • puddles of tempera paints in a shallow tray • large paper taped to workspace

Materials for Day 3 | old white socks (12 or more) • food coloring or liquid watercolors • cups, spoon or eyedropper • newspaper balls • yarn or needle and thread (adult step) • scissors • more yarn

Materials for Day 4 | good socks, to be decorated and worn • heavy paper or cardboard • scissors • acrylic or fabric paints • pencil with eraser • printing objects (see Day 4 for ideas) • optional—puffy paints from a craft store

Materials for Day 5 | socks (any kind or size) • poster board or cardstock rectangle • child's plastic darning needle, and heavy thread or embroidery floss • fabric glue, tacky glue, or craft adhesive • collage materials (see Day 5 for ideas)

DAY 1

Sock Whapper Painting

- Fill an old sock half-full with sand or lightweight gravel, and tie it tightly with yarn to close. **Hint:** Sewing the sock closed is a smart idea.
- Pour puddles of tempera paint in well-washed Styrofoam trays or another shallow tray.
- Cover a work surface with newspaper. Place a large sheet of paper in the middle of the work surface. Tape the corners to the work surface to keep the paper stationary.
- Press the sock into the paint, lift it, and swing or whap it on the paper to produce a print. Consider repeating with more colors. Some artists like to hold their painted socks above the paper and simply drop them on the paper. WHAP! This creates a different and interesting kind of print.
  Note: Thin paint splashes more than thick paint, but both are messy. Be prepared. Work outdoors, work within the confines of a large cardboard box, or prepare the work area (and clothes!) for splatters.

DAY 2

Sock Mitten Painter

- Ask an adult to help you make a Sock Mitten Painter by sewing some cut-away sections of an old kitchen sponge onto two old socks. To do this, thread a piece of yarn on a large needle, push through the sponge, in and out of the sock, and back through the sponge. Tie the yarn to hold. Cover the sock with as many sponge pieces as desired. (If no sponges are available, sew on pieces of felt or other materials like scraps of an old wool sweater or pieces of leather.)

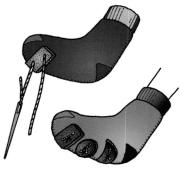

- Pour paint into a shallow tray. Slip a sock on each hand like mittens. Dip or press the socks into the paint, and then press on paper. Work as though you are fingerpainting, smearing this way and that, or make "prints" from the sponges and socks by lifting them up and down. The idea is to explore painting with your hands covered in artsy socks, so try a variety of painting methods and mixing colors.
- When done, wash the socks in the washer on cool-gentle, or simply rinse and squeeze them in the sink under running water.

Sock Ball Sculpture

- Drip food coloring or liquid watercolors on an old white sock. Repeat this for about 12 socks (or even more)!
- When the socks are dry enough to handle, stuff them with newspaper or other stuffing materials (more old socks?). Tie the top openings of the socks with yarn (or stitch them closed).
- Tie the yarn tops of all the socks together to create a large pompom style sculpture. Hang and enjoy viewing your Sock Ball Sculpture.

Wearable Dotty-Sock Craft

- Socks are easy to decorate with unique paint-dot designs. To prepare a sock, first slip a piece of heavy paper or cardboard inside the sock to prevent paint from leaking through from one side to another.
- An easy decoration method is to dip the eraser of a pencil in acrylic or fabric paint and then dab the eraser on the sock to make a dot or several dots. Repeat dipping and dotting, filling the sock with dot designs and changing colors as often as needed. Other printing items to consider include corks, sponges, or stencils. (Look around for things that will make prints.)
- When done, allow a few days for the socks to dry.
  Note: The designs will last for a long time when washed inside-out in cool water.
- ***Non-Slip Socks Idea:*** Use Puffy Paints from a craft store on the bottoms of socks to create socks that are non-slip.

One-of-a-Kind Sock Puppet

- Make a unique sock puppet with an old sock and collage materials. Choose a sock, anything from baby socks to adult socks. To make it easier to decorate, first slip a poster board or cardstock rectangle inside the sock.
- Decorate the sock in any way using collage materials. Consider sewing items to the sock with yarn or heavy thread and a large plastic darning needle, or try gluing items on the sock with tacky glue or a craft glue suitable for fabrics (Sobo® glue, Tacky® glue). Googly eyes will stick with the same glue. Glue or sew on button eyes. You can make hair from feathers, faux fur, yarn, or a chunk of old feather boa. A pompom or button works great for a nose. Felt scraps are great to use to make features like hair, eyes, nose, mouth, tongue, ears, and so on. Use markers, especially permanent or wide markers, to add more features.
- If you used glue on the sock, take the poster board out and let the puppet dry overnight. Otherwise, start to use the puppet right away: slip the sock over your hand, and make up stories or plays for your new character.

Sponges

Use clean sponges for making prints, roll to make roller designs, or as a stamp pad.

Materials for Day 1 | flat sponge, damp • pencil or dowel • yarn • scissors • tempera paints in a shallow well-washed Styrofoam grocery tray or jar lid • heavy paper

Materials for Day 2 | flat kitchen or bath sponge • scissors • paper—choose from: heavy paper, poster board, cardboard, craft paper, butcher paper, construction paper, newspaper • clothespins (the pinching kind) • tempera paints • shallow container • scrap paper • optional—markers

Materials for Day 3 | rectangular kitchen sponge, damp • well-washed Styrofoam grocery tray • tempera paints • thumb • paper • markers

Materials for Day 4 | flat yellow sponge • scissors • pebble or stone • white glue • scrap paper or felt • yarn or pipe cleaner • heavy square of poster board

Materials for Day 5 | flat sponges (or use washed sponges from Day 2) • white wrapping tissue • liquid watercolor paints or food coloring paste • flat containers like jar lids or grocery trays • scrap paper • optional—tape, scissors, note cards

DAY 1

Rolled Sponge Prints

- Roll and bend a slightly damp sponge into a cylinder shape around a pencil or dowel. Tie it with yarn to hold.
  Note: Sponges work best if they are slightly damp, even if paint will be added.
- Pour paint into a shallow container such as a jar lid or grocery tray.
- Roll the sponge like a rolling pin in paint, and then roll it on heavy paper such as poster board, cardboard, craft paper, or butcher paper. Mix and blend several colors of paint right on the paper.

DAY 2

Traditional Sponge Print

- Try this twist on the traditional sponge print: First completely paint the base paper (poster board, cardboard, paper plate, craft paper, or other heavy paper) with tempera paint. Consider painting more than one sheet. Let all the sheets dry while you prepare the sponges.
- Use scissors to cut an old flat kitchen or bath sponge into various shapes (squares, triangles, diamonds, and so on). Pinch them with clothespins, which act as handles, or simply hold the sponges with your fingers.
- Pour paint into a shallow container such as a jar lid or grocery tray. Prepare several paint colors to encourage mixing and blending.
- Dip a slightly damp sponge piece in paint, and dab on scrap paper to remove a little excess paint. Press the sponge firmly on the painted paper or cardboard to make prints, fancy designs, or actual pictures. Repeat the printing process as desired.
  Hint: Jar lids filled with a little paint make easily controllable paint containers. Sometimes an unexpected color blending of the background paint and the sponge paint happens, which can have surprisingly positive results.
- *Marker Highlight Idea:* When the sponge art is dry, use markers (water-based or permanent) to trace around and enhance the colorful shapes.

Thumbprint Squares

- Cut paper into squares.
- A rectangular kitchen sponge becomes a stamp pad in this printing activity. To make the stamp pad, place a slightly damp sponge in a plastic grocery tray. Spread some tempera paint on the sponge. Consider placing several colors of tempera paint on the same sponge.
- To make a print, press your thumb on the paint-filled sponge, and then on a square of paper. Repeat this process, making designs with your thumbprints on the square.
- When the thumbprints are dry, use markers to add more detail.

Mouse & Sponge-Cheese

- Cut a triangle from an old yellow sponge. This is the mouse's "cheese."
- Find a small, rounded stone or large pebble to use as the mouse's body. Wash and dry the stone. Glue the stone to the sponge. It should look like a mouse sitting on a block of cheese.
- Cut little features—eyes, whiskers, ears—for the mouse from scrap paper or felt. Consider using googly eyes as well. To make a tail, glue on a strand of yarn, felt, or a pipe cleaner under the back edge of the stone mouse.
- When the mouse is finished, glue the Mouse & Sponge-Cheese to a heavy square of poster board.

Tissue Sponge Dye

- Cut sponges into various shapes, or use the pre-cut sponges from Day 2 (first wash the sponges to remove excess paint).
- Lay out paper or newspaper to cover your workspace and also to absorb extra paint color. Spread white wrapping tissue on the workspace. Pat and smooth out the folds or wrinkles, if any.
- Pour several different colors of liquid watercolor paints into different flat containers like jar lids or grocery trays. You can use paste food coloring mixed with water if you do not have liquid watercolors.
- Dip the bottom of a slightly damp sponge into one color of paint, dab on a scrap of paper to remove excess paint, and then stamp it on the white tissue paper in any design. Usually a sponge will make more than one print before re-dipping it into more paint. Try dipping sponge shapes in more than one color as well as adding more shapes and designs in any way.
- When the tissue is covered in bright designs, let it dry. The tissue can be used many ways, including:
  - Tape it in a window to show off the designs and colors.
  - Use the tissue for wrapping paper.
  - Cut the tissue into smaller pieces to decorate note cards.

Stickers

Materials for Day 1 | sticker dots, any color • large sheet of plain paper • markers

Materials for Day 2 | stickers of all kinds (about 100): special stickers, sticker dots, gold or silver foil stars, stickers with pictures, and any other stickers • foam core board • yardstick, and pencil or marker • blue painter's masking tape • liquid watercolors in a hand-held spray bottle (or paintbrushes) • ruler or spatula (straight edge) • paper towels • optional—metallic gold or silver pen

Materials for Day 3 | gold or silver foil stars • black or dark blue tempera paint, paintbrush • optional—black or blue construction paper • shoebox • scissors • aluminum foil • glue or tape • cutouts (see Day 3 for ideas) • yarn, string, or thread • optional—flashlight

Materials for Day 4 | ingredients and materials for Sticker Sugar-Glue: bowl, spoon, saucepan, stove (adult step), unflavored gelatin, cold water, boiling water, corn syrup, lemon extract • paintbrush • markers or crayons • drawing paper • used greeting cards or extra photographs • scissors • waxed paper or newspaper

Materials for Day 5 | stickers of any kind: sticker dots, stars, picture-stickers, home-made stickers, and so on • yarn • scissors • collage materials • colored paper scraps, ribbon, plastic snap-on lid with holes punched in the edge • stapler, tape, or glue

DAY 1

Sticker Dots Loopy Do

- Ask an adult to help you tack or tape a large sheet of plain paper to the wall or on a paint easel.
- Press a sticker dot on the paper. Add more and more sticker dots in any pattern, leaving white space in between the sticker dots. (You may want to let some stickers overlap here and there.)
- When your sticker design is complete, take a colored marker and draw a line that will loop between the sticker dots around and around the paper.
- Select a different color marker and add more loops around the sticker dots. Fill the paper with happy colorful loops around colorful dots.

DAY 2

Favorite Sticker Mini-Masterpieces

- Sometimes stickers are so special they can be displayed and admired as mini-artworks. Ask an adult to help you section off a grid on a piece of foam-core board. Make as many squares as you have stickers. Make the squares about 2"–3" square. Not sure how many stickers to plan for? Make a grid that is 10 squares by 10 squares, making 100 total squares.
- Place blue painters' tape to form the grid lines.
- Spray liquid watercolors from hand-held misting bottles, one color per bottle. If you do not have a spray bottle available, paint liquid watercolors all over the board with a wide brush. Use a ruler or spatula to spread the wet paint around, over the tape.
- Blot up extra moisture with an old towel or paper towels. Dry briefly.
- Pull off all the tape, and you will have a board with white lines that divide the colored squares.
- Stick one special sticker in each space. Fill any empty spaces one sticker at a time as new special stickers come along. For additional special decoration, draw around the most special stickers with a metallic gold or silver pen.

Starry Night Box

- Paint the inside of a shoebox with black or dark blue tempera paint, or cover the inside of the box by gluing black or dark blue construction paper on all the surfaces.
- Turn the box on its side like a stage. Attach foil stars to the background of the box. If desired, cut a moon from aluminum foil or use a shiny large foil sticker to stick into the night sky. The scene that will fill the box is entirely up to you, the artist. Consider adding some of the following ideas to create a scene: cutouts from magazines or catalogs, cutout scenes or people from greeting cards, small plastic toys, toys or cutouts hanging from the ceiling of the box on thread or yarn, small artificial flower blossoms, cutouts from photographs, dollhouse furniture or people.
- Use scissors, tape, and glue to create the scene in your Starry Night Box. For extra drama, turn out the lights and shine a flashlight into the box to light up your Starry Night Box scene.

Old-Fashioned Stickers

- Old-fashioned stickers were a real a lick-and-stick experience, not the quick peel-and-stick convenience of today's stickers.
- To make old-fashioned stickers, ask an adult to help you make tasty Sticker Sugar-Glue: In a small bowl, sprinkle 1 packet (¼ ounce) unflavored gelatin (Knox® is a good brand to use) into 1 tablespoon cold water. Set aside until the gelatin softens. An adult can pour the softened gelatin into a small saucepan with 3 tablespoons boiling water. Stir until completely dissolved. Add ½ teaspoon corn syrup and ½ teaspoon lemon extract (or any other flavored extract). Mix thoroughly.
- Make pictures for stickers by drawing with markers or crayons on drawing paper, or by cutting out parts of your favorite greeting cards or photographs. When cutting, highlight the most interesting subject or part of the card.
- Brush the Sticker Sugar-Glue on the back of all your stickers, and let them dry face down (Sticker Sugar-Glue side up) on waxed paper or newspaper. After they are dry, save them in a dry plastic bag until you are ready to use them. Then, simply lick or moisten a sticker and apply to paper.

Sticker Dot Garland

- Cut a 6'–12' long piece of yarn and stretch it out on the floor or a work table.
- Choose two sticker dots (or two medium-to-large stickers of any kind) and press the two stickers together with the yarn sandwiched in between. (Consider using two of the Old-Fashioned Stickers from Day 4.) Repeat the sandwiching of stickers all along the length of yarn at various intervals.
- When the yarn is decorated from one end to the other, hang it like a garland over a door or window. Some artists like to tape, tie, or glue other collage materials to the yarn between the stickers; other artists like to cut out colored paper shapes and staple or glue these on the yarn.
- Consider making more than one garland, and tie each successive garland to the first to make a very long Sticker Dot Garland.
- *Ribbon Mobile Idea:* Do the same sandwiching of two stickers along ribbons, instead of yarn, and then tie the ribbons to holes that are punched around the edge of a plastic lid. Add another ribbon to make a loop on the top of the lid, and hang this mobile from a high place.

Stickers

Styrofoam

Styrofoam® comes in many shapes, thicknesses, products, and uses. This week includes artwork using five different kinds of Styrofoam®.

Materials for Day 1 | Styrofoam packing block • items to insert in the Styrofoam (see Day 1 for ideas) • lightweight hammer, or wooden mallet • yarn, string, or ribbon • scissors

Materials for Day 2 | Styrofoam sheet or block • aluminum foil • scissors • pipe cleaners and craft wire • collage items with holes—choose from: drinking straw segments, beads, buttons • cookie sheet or cutting board • optional—tissue paper scraps and tape

Materials for Day 3 | Styrofoam grocery tray (well-washed) • pencil • tempera paint on a cookie sheet or cutting board • craft roller (brayer from craft or art store) • paper optional—additional Styrofoam grocery tray, corrugated cardboard, glue, nail, scissors with points • optional—nail or scissors point

Materials for Day 4 | Styrofoam cup • permanent marker • potting soil or dirt, and grass seed • scissors • window with light, water, newspaper

Materials for Day 5 | foam-core board (Styrofoam layer between papers layers) • scissors • watercolor paints and brush, or markers • toothpicks • tape and glue

DAY 1

Hammer-It Block Sculpture

- Hammer a selection of straight items into a Styrofoam block. Good choices include golf tees, chopsticks, toy pegs (and nails, with adult supervision). Pipe cleaners and wire can be inserted by hand.
- For added color and design, wrap yarn, string, or ribbon around and around the items, wrapping from one peg to the next until the sculpture is complete.

DAY 2

Foil & Wire Sculpture

- Wrap a Styrofoam sheet or block in aluminum foil to keep the Styrofoam from breaking down.
- Stick pipe cleaners and craft wire into the Styrofoam to build a sculpture. Slip beads, buttons, and other collage items with holes onto the wires. Wires can be bent, curled, and joined together in fun ways. Also consider taping little pieces of tissue and paper to the wires to add color and design.

Foam Prints

- Cut the edges from a grocery tray to make a flat piece of Styrofoam.
- With a pencil, draw on the flat Styrofoam. Use the pencil to press the drawing deep into the Styrofoam. Some artists draw lines into the Styrofoam, and others push the Styrofoam down so the lines will be raised. Experiment a little and see the difference.
  Note: Whatever the image, remember that printing it will show the reverse.
- Squeeze some paint on a cookie sheet or a cutting board. Smooth the paint with the craft roller, and then roll paint onto the drawing.
- Press a sheet of paper on the drawing, patting it and rubbing it gently. Then peel away the paper to see the print.
- Try the following ideas:
  - *Raised Foam Print:* Cut pieces of Styrofoam from a second tray and glue them on the first tray. Use this to make prints. The raised designs will print clearly.
  - *Cardboard Print:* With adult supervision, cut designs in the top layer of corrugated cardboard using a nail or the points of scissors. Then peel those pieces away revealing the bumpy cardboard underneath. Make prints the same way as with Foam Prints, using a roller (brayer) and paint to make a print.

Hairy Funny Face Craft

- Use a permanent marker to draw a funny face on a white Styrofoam cup. It can be a person, an animal, or an imaginary creature. The cup character will have green hair growing from its head when the activity is complete!
- Fill the cup at least ¾ full with dirt. Sprinkle the dirt with grass seed. (Chia watercress, catnip, wheat grass, and barley also work instead of grass seed.)
- Place the container on a saucer or tray in a window area where it will receive indirect light. Water the seeds. Keep an eye on the cup every day to see if the green hair (grass) is growing.
- When the hair is standing well above the cup's edge, place the cup on a sheet of newspaper and cut the hair. Some artists prefer to let the hair grow and grow and never cut it. Enjoy how the cup-character changes as its hair grows.

Foam-Core Sculpture

- Foam-core board has shiny paper layers on the outside, with Styrofoam sandwiched in between on the inside. Cut it into squares about 3"–4" wide.
- Paint or decorate the squares with watercolor paints or markers before beginning the sculpture. Drying time will be short.
- To build a sculpture, stick toothpicks into one foam-core square, and then stick the other end of the same toothpick into a second square, to join the two pieces together. One end of the toothpick in one square and the other end in a different square will bring the squares together quickly as the sculpture grows in size and design. Try to keep the sculpture balanced so it will stand.
- Use tape or glue instead of or in addition to toothpicks if needed. The ultimate size of a Foam-Core Sculpture depends on how many squares there are to work with, and the imagination and determination of the artist.

Tin Cans

Simple tin cans transform easily into special art projects.

Materials for Day 1 | cans, choose from: coffee can, soup can, tuna can, cat food can, other cans • yarn • tempera paints in a shallow tray or pan • large paper • optional thick collage materials (see Day 1 for ideas)

Materials for Day 2 | coffee can, with lid • paper • golf balls, one for each color of paint • tempera paints in small bowls • spoons • tray • optional—marbles or other round balls or objects

Materials for Day 3 | tuna cans or shallow cat food cans • square board • glue, tape • optional—hammer and nail (adult step) • liquid watercolors and brush, or fabric and glue • scissors • to decorate the cans—(see Day 3 for ideas) • optional—clear plastic wrap, rubber band or clear tape

Materials for Day 4 | can or container—choose from: soup, coffee, Pringles® or round oatmeal container • thinned white glue and a brush (or hobby coating like Mod Podge®) • items to place in container, such as: loose items for crafts or sewing, pencils, dried flowers, and other storage and display ideas

Materials for Day 5 | medium-sized can • hammer • nail • sidewalk or other durable work surface • yarn • acrylic or BioColor® paints (sticks to cans well) • paintbrushes • optional—glitter glue • collage items (see Day 5 for ideas)

DAY 1

We Can Print

- Wrap yarn around a can in any design. The yarn can crisscross over itself as you wrap it. Or you can wrap it in a single spiral. Any wrapping design will work. Tie the loose ends of the yarn tightly around the can when the wrapping is complete.
- Fill a shallow tray or pan with tempera paint. Pouring paint on a pad of damp paper towels in the pan will also produce a good printing result.
- To make We Can Prints, roll the yarn-wrapped can in the shallow tray of paint, and then roll it on large paper. The lines from the yarn will make designs as the can is rolled this way and that. Roll the can in several different colors to mix colors and designs.
- *Rolled Prints Idea:* Glue thick items to a can and make rolled prints. Good materials to glue or tape to the can include pieces of Styrofoam, adhesive bandages, bunion pads, and small cardboard pieces. **Note:** Check all cans carefully. Cover any sharp edges with duct tape.

DAY 2

Roly-Poly Can

- Ask an adult to pre-cut drawing paper to fit inside a coffee can. Keep a stack of the paper handy. Roll and slip a sheet of paper into a coffee can so the paper unrolls and lines the can.
- Place a golf ball in a small bowl of thin tempera paint. Several bowls of paint, each with one golf ball, increase the color options. Roll the ball around with a spoon to coat it with paint.
- Choose two colors (balls) and transfer both into the coffee can with the spoon. Snap on the lid. Shake the can gently, or for more fun, two children can roll the can back and forth between them.
- When ready, open the can and pour the balls on a tray (then rinse, dry, and replace in the bowls of paint). Remove the paper and see the design that you created. Add a new sheet of paper and create another design. If golf balls are not available, use marbles or other round objects or balls. **Note:** Check all cans carefully. Cover any sharp edges with duct tape.

DAY 3

Tuna Can Collection

- Save tuna cans. (Cat food cans are also great for this project.) Wash and dry cans thoroughly, removing the labels. An adult can cover sharp edges with duct tape, although most cans have smooth edges.
- Arrange the cans on a board and glue in place. If you prefer, hammer a nail (with adult supervision) through the can and into the board for stronger results. The board can be left plain or pre-painted or covered with fabric.
- You can decorate the cans by wrapping them with paper. Use strips of construction paper, wrapping paper, magazine pictures, or other patterned paper. Secure with a little glue or a piece of tape.
- To show off a Tuna Can Collection, glue a special object in each can, such as a special rock, shell, fancy bead or button, dried flower, or any other special object. Little drawings or photos could also fill each can.
- *Clear Peek Idea:* Cover each can with a piece of clear plastic wrap and secure tightly with a rubber band or clear tape.

DAY 4

Découpage Can Craft

- Get ready to wrap a picture around any kind of can or container. Suitable containers are those from soup, coffee, or even a Pringles or round oatmeal container. Draw or color a picture on thick paper that will fit around the container.
- Brush the entire back of the picture with thinned white glue or a hobby coating like Mod Podge®, and then wrap the picture all the way around the container, pressing to hold. Dry for about two hours.
- Coat the entire picture with another layer of thin white glue or Mod Podge®. Let this dry overnight (or another full day, if possible). Another layer will add an extra thick shine, but one layer will do very nicely.
- Containers with lids are great to store loose items for crafts or sewing; containers without lids are perfect for pencils, dried flowers, and for display options.

DAY 5

Smashed Tin-Can Sculpture

- Ask an adult to pound two small holes about 1" apart in the side of a medium-sized can near the top opening. You will tie yarn through the holes to display the sculpture.
- To smash the can, place it on its side on a sidewalk or other hard surface.
  Note: Try to have the two holes in the can against the sidewalk.
- **Adult help required:** To flatten the can, strike the hammer down firmly on the top of the can in the middle. The bottom part will bend forward. Then step on the can to bend the round bottom part further against the rest of the can.
- Paint the can with acrylic or BioColor® paint. Add glitter glue if desired. To make the can into an interesting sculpture, select items to slip inside and protrude from the can. Some suggestions are Popsicle sticks, chopsticks, bamboo skewers, twigs, old pencils, and artificial flowers. Decorate these "sticks" with paper scraps, ribbons, bottle caps, costume jewelry, corks, lids, felt shapes, or small toys or party favors.
- Tie yarn through the two holes and hang the sculpture.

Tin Cans

Toys

Materials for Day 1 | tricycle or bicycle tire • large sheet of paper on the floor or a flat surface outdoors • tempera paint in a large tray • optional—marbles, paper, cake pan; toy car, tempera paints, paper towels

Materials for Day 2 | ABC magnets • sheet of tagboard • pencil • circle template (the diameter should be about the same width as the width of the ABC magnets) • markers, crayons, colored pencils, scissors • glue or tape • metal surface, like a refrigerator door

Materials for Day 3 | selection of small toys • cardboard box or table top (for display) • scenery ideas (see Day 3 for ideas) • optional—digital camera

Materials for Day 4 | matboard frames, pre-cut (or a hand-cut cardboard frame) • scissors • painting or coloring ideas: tempera paints, watercolor paints, colored chalk • paintbrushes or tissue • small stray or broken toys (see Day 4 for ideas) • white glue (glue gun, adult only) • photograph or original artwork to fit in the frame • paper clip, duct tape

Materials for Day 5 | small loose toys, small stray or broken toys, parts of toys (checkers, buttons, puzzle pieces) • optional—small cardboard shapes • white glue • square of wood or cardboard • acrylic paints and paintbrushes

DAY 1

Tire-Tread Prints

- Use a full-size tricycle tire to make prints! Spread a large piece of paper on the floor or outdoors on the ground.
- Fill one large tray with tempera paint, or make several trays with different colors. Fill a plastic tub with water, and have an old towel handy.
- Holding both sides of the tire in the center, roll the tire through a tray of paint, turning the tire by hand to be sure that the paint covers the entire tire tread. Now roll the tire across the large paper, leaving a tread print. Change colors and repeat.
  Note: Consider rinsing and drying the tire between applying colors to it, or simply allow color mixing without worry. Both ways produce clear and interesting tread prints.
- Other toys or wheels that make interesting or surprising prints:
  ○ *Quick Marble Art Idea:* Place a marble in a shallow cup of paint and then plop on top of a circle of paper in a cake pan. You might want to put additional marbles in the same pan. Tip the pan this way and that, rolling the marbles around to make prints on the paper.
  ○ *Quick Toy Car Art Idea:* Drive a small toy car or little wheeled toy through paint poured on a pad of paper towels, and then drive the car on large paper to make wheel prints in many colors.

DAY 2

ABC Magnet Art

- Spread out ABC magnets on a sheet of tagboard. Trace one circle for each magnet; the circles should be a little bit bigger than the magnets.
- In each circle, draw a mini-artwork, design, or pattern with markers or crayons. Fill each circle in any way.
  Hint: Consider coloring outside the lines and larger than the circle because the marks outside the circle will be cut away.
- Cut out all the circles. Glue or tape one art circle to each ABC magnet. (Pressing a loop of tape on the circle and then on the magnet is an easy way to temporarily attach the art to the letter.)
- Stick the new art magnets to the fridge and enjoy moving them around in different patterns and arrangements.

DAY 3

Toy Scene Arrangement

- Find an area where a Toy Scene Arrangement can be set up for a week or so. Using the top of a cardboard box or table in the corner of a room is perfect.
- Arrange your favorite toys in a scene that communicates a simple story or is interesting to view. Many artists like to create a humorous scene. For example, have a teddy bear ride on the back of a piggy bank, a doll hold a toy stuffed kitten on her lap, a toy fire engine go to a Lego® house that has paper flames taped to it, and so on.
- Arranging scenes is a highly creative and imaginative experience. Props of all kinds, including things cut from colored paper, can enhance the scene. Some artists like to take photographs of their scenes to talk about and enjoy after they disassemble them.

DAY 4

Toy-Inspired Frame Craft

- Frame shops usually have matboard pre-cut as frames that they may give to you. If a matboard frame is not available, ask an adult to cut a simple frame from a rectangle of cardboard. This will work just as well. Simply cut out the center from the cardboard rectangle.
- Ideas to decorate the matboard or cardboard frame include:
  - Paint it with tempera paints, and allow it to dry.
  - Paint it with watercolor paints, and allow it to dry.
  - Color it with colored chalk and then rub and rub it with tissue until the color is polished and no longer smudgy.
  - Leave it uncolored.
- Spread small stray toys, puzzle pieces, marbles, pegs, checkers, and other small parts of toys on your workspace. Choose some of the toys to glue to the frame. Cover the frame entirely, or add only a few toys or toy pieces in a carefully planned design.
- When the glue is dry, tape a photograph or original artwork to the back of the frame so the image shows through the opening to the front.
- To hang the frame, you can make a simple hook device by taping a paper clip to the back upper center of the frame with duct tape.

DAY 5

Assembled Toy Relief

- Save small loose toys, lost toys, broken small pieces of toys, or toy parts to create an assembled relief. (A relief is a textured flat sculpture where the design stands out from the surface.) Gather other pieces like checkers, buttons, puzzle pieces, or small squares of cardboard too.
- Glue a selection of toys and other pieces on a square of wood or cardboard. Fill the square completely using a lot of white glue. Feel free to layer or overlap the pieces. Let the glue dry overnight.
- When dry, paint the entire assembled relief with acrylic paint so the art is shiny and all the pieces become part of one textured relief. White or black paint is a good choice for a traditional artistic relief, but some artists prefer using bright colors or multi-colored designs.

Waxed Paper

Waxed paper is itself a unique art material. It is also an important foundation in assisting with the creation of artwork that requires a non-stick base.

Material for Day 1 | waxed paper • white glue in squeeze bottle • glitter, colored salt, or colored sand • thread or yarn • scissors • optional– tempera, watercolors or food coloring, toothpicks

Material for Day 2 | waxed paper • white glue in a squeeze bottle • yarn • scissors • white glue thinned with water • glitter or bits of art tissue • scissors • paper clip and yarn

Material for Day 3 | scissors • waxed paper • salad oil or baby oil in a cup • cotton ball • art tissue scraps, any colors

Material for Day 4 | waxed paper • thick towel • ironing board • newsprint • old cheese grater • peeled crayon stubs • optional—very small items like confetti, hole-punch dots, leaves • iron (adult only) • scissors • tape

Material for Day 5 | waxed paper • white glue mixed with food coloring in a shallow cup • flat collage materials—choose from: paper doilies, torn or cut pieces of art tissue, tissue pieces, small paper shapes, leaves or flat blossoms, bits of foil, snips of ribbon, clippings from magazines or gift wrap paper • scissors • hole punch, yarn, staple (or tape)

DAY 1

One Line Peely Glue

- Squeeze white glue on waxed paper in one very long and continuous line. Sprinkle with glitter, colored salt, or colored sand. The glue must dry until Day 5 of this week.
- On Day 5, peel the glue design from the waxed paper and hang it by a thread or strand of yarn. **Note:** White glue dries clear.
- *Colored Glue Idea:* Mix glue with tempera paint, liquid watercolors, or food coloring in shallow cups. Drip colored glue on waxed paper in bold solid shapes with plastic spoons or craft sticks. Use a toothpick to make a hole so you can hang these shapes when they are dry. Dry until Day 5. Peel the colored glue designs carefully from the waxed paper. String the designs on yarn and hang them from a stick, or glue them onto colored paper.

DAY 2

Waxed Paper Yarn

- Squeeze a line of glue on waxed paper, creating a closed shape, which is a shape where the line connects from start to finish, like a circle or square, not an open shape like a squiggle.
- Push yarn into the glue line so the ends of the yarn connect. Make several shapes with glue and yarn on the waxed paper.
- Paint a little glue that has been thinned with water inside the yarn shapes. Sprinkle glitter or bits of art tissue inside the shapes. Let the shapes dry overnight until Day 3.
- Cut around the outside of the yarn shapes on Day 3. The center of the yarn shape will be decorated.
- Poke a hole and insert a bent paper clip in the shape; hang to display.

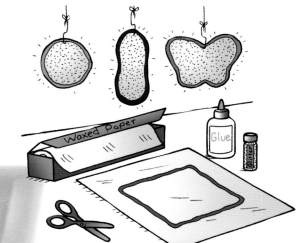

Oil & Tissue Explore

Reminder: Today is the day to cut out the yarn shapes made on Day 2. (See Day 2 for directions.)

- Pour a few tablespoons of salad oil or baby oil in a shallow cup. Cover your workspace with protective paper.
- Dip a cotton ball in the oil and brush it back and forth across a sheet of waxed paper, covering the paper, and leaving a border, if possible, for ease of handling.
- Tear colorful art-tissue scraps into pieces and press them on the oiled, waxed paper. The tissue pieces will stick in the oil and become bright and translucent. You may need to dab the tissue pieces with a little more oil (use the cotton ball).
- Display in a window, if desired.
- Use plenty of soap and water for clean up.
  Note: The oil will never quite dry, so display these pieces where oil will not be a problem.

Traditional Crayon Melt

- Tear off two sheets of waxed paper from the roll. The sheets should be the same size. Fold a thick towel in half and place it on a table as an ironing board. Put a sheet of newsprint over the towel. Place one piece of waxed paper on the paper.
- Using an old cheese grater reserved especially for art, grate peeled crayon stubs into shavings and let them fall onto the waxed paper. (An adult should help with this step.) Spread the shavings around the waxed paper until you are satisfied with the design. Consider adding other small items like confetti, hole-punch dots, or even a leaf or two.
- Place a second sheet of waxed paper over the crayon shavings. Cover this with plain paper or newsprint. Ask an adult to quickly and firmly press a warm iron (no steam) on this stack of papers. This warms the crayon shavings and waxed paper and begins the melting process. Peek to see how things are going. It should not take long before the wax melts.
- Allow the creation to cool a little, and then remove it from the ironing area. Trim the edges of the waxed paper or cut it into wide strips for hanging. Some artists like to feel how the waxed paper has become "crisp." Crayon Melts are always pretty when you hang them in a sunny window where the colors can glow brightly.

Glue Sandwich

Reminder: Today is the day to peel the glue design from the waxed paper from Day 1. (See Day 1 for directions.)

- Begin the Glue Sandwich. Mix white glue with paint or food coloring in a shallow cup to create a bright color. Make several colors.
- Fold a sheet of waxed paper in half, and then unfold it. Use a paintbrush to apply colored glue on one side of the waxed paper.
- Stick thin, flat materials to the glue on the waxed paper. Some ideas include: pieces of paper doilies, torn or cut pieces of art tissue, pieces of other kinds of tissue, small paper shapes, leaves or flat blossoms, bits of foil, snips of ribbon, and small clippings from magazines or gift wrap paper.
- Fold the second side of the waxed paper over the first, and press with your hands to seal the glue and flat items inside. Dry briefly. Trim the edges.
- To hang or display the Glue Sandwich, punch holes through the top edge of the artwork and tie yarn through them, or staple a yarn loop to the artwork. Tape will also work well instead of staples. Display the artwork in a window or near a light source.

Waxed Paper

Wrapping Tissue

Wrinkled or torn white tissue papers are just as usable as brand new sheets for creating wonderful art.

Materials for Day 1 | white tissue paper (uncoated and absorbent, not the shiny coated kind) • clean newsprint or a plastic tablecloth • piece of damp sponge • liquid watercolors in a shallow tray • paper towels • optional—iron (for adult use only) • optional— printing items (see Day 1 for ideas)

Materials for Day 2 | white tissue paper (uncoated and absorbent, not the shiny coated kind) • tempera paint in a shallow tray • plain newsprint or butcher paper • optional—scrunched balls of newspaper

Materials for Day 3 | white tissue paper (uncoated and absorbent, not the shiny coated kind) • matboard or foam core board square • water and a paintbrush or sponge • liquid watercolors in the cups of a muffin tin • optional—decorate with markers, paint, pens, or more liquid watercolors

Materials for Day 4 | white tissue paper cut into circles (squares work too) • scissors • decorating supplies (see Day 4 for ideas) • pipe cleaners • plastic soda straws • choose a vase: baby food jar, soup can, yogurt container • decorating materials (see Day 4 for ideas) • optional—gravel, sand, or a lump of playdough

Materials for Day 5 | tagboard, thin cardboard, or paper plates • scissors • large white background • paper (see Day 5 for ideas) • liquid watercolors and paintbrushes • thinned white glue and brush • large sheet of white wrapping tissue

DAY 1

Sponge-Printed Tissue

- Fold a large sheet of white tissue in half and then fold in half again. Place it on clean newsprint or on a plastic table cover.
- Pinch a piece of damp sponge between two fingers, dip the sponge in liquid watercolors, and then gently and quickly dab the sponge on the tissue. The color will soak in quickly, so do not press too hard or too long in one spot. The color will soak through the layers of tissue so all four sides will have similar designs.
- Create more dabs and prints all over the paper. Let the paper dry on the table until it can be handled easily. Soak up any puddles of color with paper towels or an art towel.
- When dry enough to handle, move the tissue to a drying space for a little longer. Unfold when dry. If you want the wrinkles in the paper removed, ask an adult to iron the tissue on low heat, no steam. Many artists prefer the wrinkled feeling and look. Enjoy the Sponge-Printed Tissue as art, or use it for wrapping paper.
Note: Use other items to make prints, like plastic alphabet letters, kitchen utensils, corks, and so on. The wrapping tissue may also be printed on when not folded, but use liquid colors sparingly so the paper doesn't become too soaked and tear.

DAY 2

Tissue-Scrunch Printing

- Scrunch a large sheet of white tissue paper into a fluffy ball or wad. Pinch the ball of tissue paper between your fingers, and press it into a very shallow tray of tempera paint.
- Press the tissue paper ball on a large sheet of plain newsprint or butcher paper to make a print. You should be able to make several prints before needing to dip the tissue paper ball back into the paint.
- Make several balls of tissue paper, one for each color of paint. Continue creating more prints, overlapping colors and filling the paper in any way. Change balls of tissue paper often. Some artists say the prints remind them of flower blossoms. You can save and dry the soaked balls of tissue paper for other art projects.
Note: Try using scrunched balls of newspaper to create an interesting print variation.
Hint: White tissue works best if it is the ordinary plain, soft white tissue paper, not the coated or shiny variety.

Tissue-Covered Painting

- First soak a square of matboard or foam-core board with water so it is moist. Place a sheet of white tissue paper on the wet board. Use a paintbrush or sponge to gently brush a little more water on the tissue paper to even out the moisture. The tissue paper will become very wrinkly and bumpy.
- Drip, dab, or brush liquid watercolors freely on the wet tissue paper, letting colors mix and blend. Let the painting dry.
- Remove and discard the tissue paper, noticing how it has made designs and patterns on the board. The painting is complete. However, you may wish to add more designs and embellishments with markers, paint, pens, or more watercolors.

Easy Tissue Flowers Craft

- Cut white tissue paper into circles (squares work too). Spread the tissue circles out on a covered workspace where you can decorate each circle.
- Choose a method for decorating the tissue paper circles. Some ideas include:
    - Make dots with markers.
    - Drip paint from a brush.
    - Fold into smaller shapes and dip in food coloring mixed with water.
    - Spray with liquid watercolor from a hand-mister.
    - Dab with sponges or other items dipped in paint.
    - Dab with glitter glue.
    - Dot with white glue and sprinkle with confetti.
- When dry, crumple the circle in the center and "tie" it with a pipe cleaner to make a blossom. The pipe cleaner will be the stem. For extra strength, slip the pipe cleaner into a plastic soda straw.
- Place the flower in any type of "vase," such as a baby food jar, soup can, or yogurt container. Decorate the container by covering it with aluminum foil, wrapping paper, or construction paper.
  Hint: Add gravel, sand, or a lump of playdough at the bottom of lightweight vases so they are less likely to tip over.

Tissue-Covered Relief

- Cut heavy paper (tagboard, thin cardboard, or paper plates) into shapes.
- Glue the heavy paper shapes on a piece of white butcher paper, drawing paper, the back of an old white poster, or white cardboard. Fill the paper with shapes and then let the shapes dry briefly so they are stable. This is called a relief.
- Paint the relief with liquid watercolors. (Liquid watercolors will soak into heavy papers very quickly.)
- Brush white glue thinned with water over the entire relief.
- Before the glue dries, place a sheet of white wrapping tissue over the relief. Brush it in place with a little more white glue thinned with water. (Some artists simply pat the tissue in place rather than brush it with glue.) The tissue will become wrinkled and bumpy.
- Tuck the loose edges of the tissue to the back of the paper, or trim the edges. Dry completely, and enjoy.

Wrapping Tissue

Yarn

Yarn is an exciting material because it comes in so many interesting colors and textures, from variegated to fuzzy, soft to firm, thin to thick, metallic to glossy.

Materials for Day 1 | yarn, 12"–18" lengths • shallow dishes of tempera paint • paintbrush • paper—choose from: cardstock or tagboard, matboard, paper plate, copier or printer paper, construction paper, other paper

Materials for Day 2 | yarn in several colors • hole-punch • scissors • art materials to work with—choose from: sturdy paper plate, board with flat headed nails

Materials for Day 3 | strands of yarn • scissors • heavy paper • white glue in a squeeze bottle • tempera paints and paintbrushes • optional—sheet of any weight paper

Materials for Day 4 | yarn • wooden spoons or other spoons (wooden ice-cream spoons from small cups of ice cream, or plastic spoons) • scissors • glue • markers • collage items (see Day 4 for ideas)

Materials for Day 5 | yarn in many colors • scissors • stick from outdoors, about 1"-2" in diameter and at least 1' long (optional: scrap of wood, dowel, broomstick, other stick) • collage items (see Day 5 for ideas)

DAY 1

Painty Yarn

- Yarn invites a variety of art explorations. Make Painty Yarn by soaking 12"–18" yarn strands in a shallow dish of paint. Here are some ideas for using Painty Yarn:
  - *Yarn Print:* Place the Painty Yarn on a sheet of paper like cardstock or tagboard. Tape the corners of the paper to the table to prevent wiggling. Place a second sheet of any kind of paper on top of the yarn. Pat it in place. Peel the top paper away to see the print.
  - *Yarn Drag Design:* Drag strands of Painty Yarn over paper to make designs, allowing different colors to mix on the paper.
  - *Folded Yarn Print:* Place a strand of Painty Yarn inside a folded sheet of paper, hold the paper down firmly with one hand, and pull the yarn out with the other. Open the folded paper to see the wiggly design. Try mixing several colored strands of yarn at once.
  - *Yarn Drop Design:* Drop Painty Yarn from above the paper, letting it land as it may. Then press and dab the yarn firmly on the paper with a paintbrush to squeeze out the paint. Lift the yarn strands from the paper and see the remaining design.

DAY 2

Three Yarn Weavings

- Weaving with yarn can be done many ways. Here are three possibilities:
  - *Punched-Plate Weaving:* Ask an adult to help pre-punch holes around the outside edge of a sturdy paper plate. (For extra-sturdy plate weaving, glue two plates together and then punch the holes around the edge. This requires a strong hole punch.) Sew or weave yarn through the holes, from one hole to another, across the plate, around and around, in and out. The randomness of the design will grow as you add more and more yarn. Shorter lengths are easiest to handle, but artists with more practice can use longer lengths. Some artists like to incorporate beads and feathers in the weaving. Tape or tie off the end pieces of yarn on the back.
  - *Cut-Plate Weaving:* Instead of punching holes, ask an adult to cut ½"-deep slits around the plate about 1" apart. Tuck yarn into slits and then weave the yarn back and forth, around and around.
  - *Nailed-Board Weaving:* Ask an adult to help you pound short nails into a flat board, any shape, leaving about ½"–1" of the nail above the wood. Nails should be about 2" or more apart so your fingers can work between the nails. Wrap and tie yarn from one nail to the next, making a weaving of sorts and filling the board. Include collage materials as desired.

DAY 3

Paint over Yarn

- Glue strands or pieces of yarn on heavy paper. Use a lot of glue so the yarn will stick well; use a lot of yarn too. Dry for several hours.
- When completely dry, paint over all the yarn with one or more colors. Cover the yarn thickly with paint. The texture of the yarn covered by paint will give the art an interesting look. Allow the artwork to dry.
- *Print Idea:* Make a print from this art while the paint is still wet. Pat a sheet of paper over the yarn art, then peel away to lift a print. You can make several prints from the same yarn-covered paint before the paint dries.

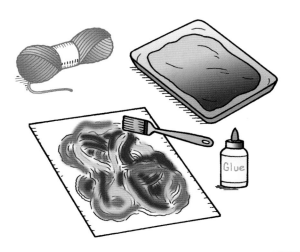

DAY 4

Spoon-Puppet

- Find an old wooden spoon or a bunch of smaller wooden ice-cream spoons. Plastic spoons work too, but they require more drying time. Gather yarn, scissors, glue, and markers. Find some collage materials, like buttons, fabric strips, feathers, paper scraps, or ribbon.
- To make a puppet or doll from a spoon, draw a face on the rounded side of the spoon with markers. Happy, sad, surprised, angry, or sleepy are some ideas for expressions.
- Glue the yarn on the top of the spoon for hair (plastic spoons may need some tape to hold the yarn until it dries). The hair can be short or long, loopy or straight. Wrap yarn around the "neck" of the puppet to add color that looks like clothing. In fact, you can wrap the entire handle in yarn, if desired. Add feathers, paper scraps, and other materials for more features and personality. It is fun to fold paper strips accordion style and attach to the spoon as silly arms or legs.
- Make a whole family of spoons, including the family spoon-pet.
- When the glue dries, have fun making the spoons talk or act out a story.
- *Storage Idea:* Stick spoon puppets all in a row in a block of Styrofoam.

DAY 5

Colorful Yarn Sticks

- Find a stick outdoors, or use a scrap of wood that is about 1"–2" wide and at least 1' long. A dowel, part of a broomstick, or any other stick will also work well. Completely cover the stick by wrapping yarn around and around it. Use many colors, and many different strands of yarn. When one strand of yarn runs out, tie it to the next strand and keep wrapping it around the stick.
- To incorporate an interesting design as you wrap the stick, tie and tuck in collage items, like ribbons, fabric strips, feathers, small toys, party favors, or buttons. If you want to display your Colorful Yarn Stick, add a long strand or loop at the end of the stick to hang it.
  Note: This artwork often takes more than one day to complete.

Zip-Close Plastic Bags

You can use every size of zip-close plastic bag to create both artwork and art-project displays.

Materials for Day 1 | large zip-close plastic bag • thick tempera paints, two colors • masking tape

Materials for Day 2 | thin zip-close sandwich bags • collage materials—choose from: lace pieces, paper doilies, bits of yarn, confetti, ribbon, pieces of foil paper, gift wrap and tissue, and so on • aluminum foil • ironing board (or padded counter or table top) • iron (adult only) • scissors

Materials for Day 3 | zip-close plastic bags of all sizes • stuffing materials (see Day 3 for ideas) • construction paper shapes or strips • scissors • optional—soda straw

Materials for Day 4 | zip-close storage plastic bags (large or medium storage size) • stapler • poster board, 2 pieces slightly larger than a bag • white paper to slip inside the bag, 2 for each bag • art materials, photographs and magazine pictures, pens or pencils

Materials for Day 5 | zip-close gallon-size plastic storage bags (about 30 total) • yarn cut into many 6" lengths • scissors • hand-held hole punch • artwork to fit in gallon bags

DAY 1

Bag Fingerpainting

- Fingerpainting in a sealable plastic bag is an inspiring way to explore colors and color mixing (red and white make pink, yellow and blue make green, and so on) with less mess. Pour a few tablespoons of one color of paint in a large zip-close plastic bag. Add a second color.
- Gently press the air out of the bag, zip it closed, and then seal it with masking tape to make sure the bag will not open.
- Press your fingers and hands on the bag, mixing and kneading the colors from outside the bag. After the colors are mixed, fingerpaint on the bag, making designs and patterns.
- **Mixing Hint:** Mixing any color with white will create a pastel shade.

DAY 2

Melted Sandwich Art

- Thin plastic sandwich bags make the best melted art bags. Arrange collage materials in a thin sandwich bag, using any selection of lace pieces, paper doilies, bits of yarn, confetti, ribbon, and pieces of foil and tissue.
- Place the bag between two pieces of aluminum foil that are a bit larger than the bag. Place the one bag sandwiched between two pieces of aluminum foil on an ironing board or on a tabletop padded with a thick, double-folded towel. Ask an adult to use a warm iron (no steam) to press the foil. Peek to see how the melting is going. The sandwich bag will melt and seal the materials inside.
- When the melting is complete and the plastic bag has cooled enough to handle, trim the edges of the bag.

Wild Puffed-Bag Art

- Any size of bag works well. Select materials with which to stuff a plastic bag. Some ideas include shredded paper, scrunched tissue, gift wrap paper scraps, ribbons, strips of plastic shopping bags, aluminum foil balls, cotton balls, fabric scraps, and so on. The bag should look wild and fun.
- Fill the bag so it is puffy, and then zip it closed. To decorate the stuffed bag in a wild way, tape other materials to the outside of the bag's edge, like colored construction paper shapes or strips. Some artists like to curl, fringe, and fold paper strips and attach these to the bag.
- *Extra Puffed Bag Idea:* Take a soda straw and insert it into the bag. Seal the bag right up to the straw, keeping the end of the straw in the bag. Blow into the straw, filling the bag with air, and then quickly pull the straw from the bag while zipping it closed as fast as possible without losing too much air. The bag will be extra puffy!

Mini-Bag Book Craft

- Stack four bags together with the open ends at the top. Staple the bags at least three times down the left side of the stack of bags to make a small "book." Ask an adult to help you staple the bags because plastic bags are slippery and hard to hold.
  Note: Make a bigger book by adding more bags to the stack.
- Cut two pieces of poster board slightly larger than the bags. Put one square on the front of the bags, and one on the back.
- Staple the left side again, from top to bottom, with many staples. (Cover the staples with duct tape to make a smooth spine for your book.) The book is now ready to fill!
- Cut white paper to fit inside the bags; cut two pieces for each bag, as each bag has a front and back for display. You can use any ideas, techniques, and methods to create art to display in the bags. Some artists like to make mini-scrapbooks with photos and magazine pictures. Others add artwork over time as they create something they would like to save. You may also wish to "write a book" with pictures, which you can insert in a certain order so they tell a story.

Stuffed Bag Quilt

Note: If you prefer a smaller bag-quilt, use half-gallon or quart-sized bags. The layout preparation requires adult help. Filling the bags with original art is up to you.

- Punch at least two holes on each side of each gallon-sized sealable plastic bag, 30 bags in all. These holes should be punched in the same places on each bag, so they can be lined up side-by-side and joined together. Keep the zip-close section intact. Do not punch holes in the zip-close section, but do punch holes just next to the "zipper" on the top edge of the bag.
- Arrange a row of five bags side-by-side on the floor or table. Place the zip-close edge at the top of the row, facing up.
- With pieces of yarn (about 6" long), lining up the punched holes side by side, tie one bag to the next in a horizontal row. Tie each bag to the one next to it to make a row, keeping the layout intact.
- Next, make a second row like the first. Attach the row to the first row, tying bags together through the punched holes with yarn as before. Continue making rows and joining rows to other rows this way until there are six rows five bags wide. The quilt is a great way to display unique artworks facing front, as well as a second artwork in each bag facing back.

Zip-Close Plastic Bags

INDEXES

Index

MATERIALS INDEX

Materials Index, by Week
(all 52 materials listed
   alphabetically, by week)

Index

Index

Index

Index

Index 127

With *First Art,* children joyfully squeeze rainbows, make their own (safe) beads to string, and create their very own painted-paper quilts. These activities start children on a journey full of exploration and creativity!
ISBN 978-0-87659-222-9
Gryphon House / 18543 / PB

The more than 200 activities in *Preschool Art* encourage children to explore and understand their world through open-ended art experiences that emphasize the process of creating art.
ISBN 978-0-87659-168-0
Gryphon House / 16985 / PB

Primary Art offers budding artists ages 5-8 more than 100 art experiences that value the process of creating art more than the final product.
ISBN 978-0-87659-283-0
Gryphon House / 17829 / PB

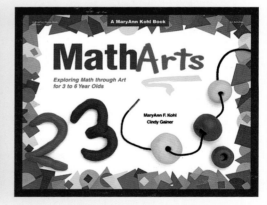

These fun, easy-to-do art activities teach children about people and cultures all over the world.
ISBN 978-0-87659-190-1
Gryphon House / 18827 / PB

The Big Messy Art Book opens the door for children to explore art on a grand, expressive scale. Children love diving into these big art experiences!
ISBN 978-0-87659-206-9
Gryphon House / 14925 / PB

MathArts is an innovative approach that uses creative art projects to introduce preschoolers to early math concepts.
ISBN 978-0-87659-177-2
Gryphon House / 16987 / PB